Declutter Your Own Spaces

With the Nine Steps to Feng Shui® System

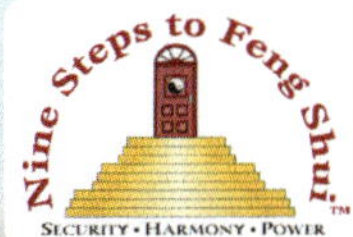

Monica P. Castaneda

Feng Shui is the ancient Chinese Art of Placement and has been in use throughout the Orient for thousands of years. The complex wisdom of the Feng Shui aspects gathered in these pages constitutes the dynamic experience of the author. An investigation of these inspired words is meant to lead you to your own understanding of this complex wisdom. The author makes no claim for absolute effectiveness. The adoption and application of the advice or information offered is solely the readers' responsibility. The author of this book does not dispense medical or psychological advice or prescribe the use of any technique as a form of treatment for medical or mental problems without the advice of a physician, either directly or indirectly. The intent of the author is only to offer information of a general nature to help readers in their quest for spiritual wellbeing. If the reader chooses to use any of the information in this book as is the reader's constitutional right, the author assumes no responsibility for the reader's actions.

Declutter Your Own Spaces with the Nine Steps to Feng Shui® System

First Edition Published April 4, 2014

ISBN-13: 978-1497548527

ISBN-10: 1497548527

For permission, contact:
Monica P. Castaneda
7786 Emory Chase Ln.
Knoxville, TN 37918

Moni@FengShuiForUs.com

www.FengShuiForUs.com

Layout and design by Monica P. Castaneda
Illustrations by Monica P. Castaneda
Public domain photos from www.publicdomainpictures.net
Stock photos from www.123rtf.com

Cover Design by Monica P. Castaneda

The Chinese say:

First, Luck

Second, Destiny

Third, Feng Shui

Fourth, Virtues

Fifth, Education

Feng Shui, the ancient art of placement, was designed thousands of years ago to help people create the conditions that can make it easier to live a good life.

Feng Shui uses the laws of nature to determine "what to put where" so you can: **Feel More Relaxed, Get Along with Others Better, Be More Productive, and Attract Greater Abundance.**

Feng Shui draws knowledge from Nature and Universal Laws in order to produce environments that promote **Wealth, Health, Love and Happiness.**

Feng Shui proposes arranging the space in order to reproduce the signs of nature that we recognize as **life-nurturing and safe.** This provides us with positive feedback about our lives.

Feng Shui can help you create a home or work environment where you can feel **safe**, in greater **harmony** with your surroundings, and in better **control** of your spaces.

“Feng Shui” means Wind and Water

The term “Feng Shui means literally “Wind and Water” the forces that shape the landscape. It is pronounced “Fung Schway” and it refers to a set of rules in Chinese philosophy that govern spatial arrangement and orientation in relation to patterns related to the Universal Laws, as expressed in the Natural World.

It is said that the term Feng Shui is actually a short way to refer to an ancient poem, which described the ideal conditions of a place where human life could thrive, in harmony with Heaven and Earth.

The winds are mild,
The sun is bright,
The water is clear,
The trees are lush.

Feng Shui is at least 5,000 years old. The Feng Shui masters of Ancient China had the responsibility of finding sites where palaces, farms, and villages could be built with a certain guarantee that people could not only survive, but prosper there. They also were to find burial sites where the memory of ancestors could be honored for generations. At a time when there were no weather reports and history had just started to be recorded, Feng Shui practitioners had to rely on their powers of observation of the natural world.

In modern times Feng Shui also deals with the surroundings of a building [including streets and other buildings], its shape and landscaping, as well as with the colors and materials of the outside and inside of a space.

Feng Shui Your Own Home offers you the opportunity to utilize the knowledge of Feng Shui without having to devote a lot of time to study.

“A loving atmosphere in your home is the foundation for your LIFE. Do all you can to create a tranquil, harmonious home.”

(Taken from the *Instructions for Life*, Author Unknown)

Table of Contents

Dealing with Clutter

Many Feng Shui consultants and teachers, as well as expert organizers talk about **getting rid** of clutter, and changing your life.

However, my experience and that of everybody else I know – especially those living in an industrialized country, is that things inside the house or workplace seem to **multiply**, as if they reproduced while we sleep... unless we are constantly letting go of the things that no longer serve us.

It would be very nice if we could just hire a cleaning and organizing team that would de-clutter our homes or offices in one day and be done with it; we wouldn't have to deal with the feelings and memories our stuff carries. We would get rid of clutter and change our lives. But what happens next? Will we just start filling up closets, drawers and cabinets again? Letting the piles of paperwork get bigger by the day... until we can no longer stand it again?

For these reasons we use the term **dealing with clutter** instead of pushing people to get rid of it.

When our spaces give us the message that "nothing is in the right place" or that "everything is a mess," this becomes constant feedback about our lives, and is not conducive to the kinds of thoughts and feelings that would put us in a position to make improvements.

Conversely, when we arrange our home and work environments to emphasize comfort, order, love and security, these will become a constant feedback to our brains and subconscious minds, which will in time translate into feelings of well being and restored confidence in the world, and hopes for the future.

Keeping Things Into Perspective

During my first few years as a Feng Shui consultant I encouraged clients to declutter from the get go.

I believed that clearing clutter was one of the first steps to take in order to improve the Feng Shui of a home, and that for other Feng Shui cures to really work, you had to declutter first.

However, after years of practice and experience I realized that clients did much better if they took care of other aspects of the Feng Shui process before addressing clutter.

When clients started decluttering too soon, we would see healing crises pop up. Some clients got dizzy while decluttering, other clients got emotional and started crying, there were even a few who felt physically ill. I used to attribute these feelings of malaise to the dust mites and other allergens that were often stirred up when moving or cleaning objects that had not been moved in a long time, but over time I realized that they were feeling dis-ease because they felt forced to do something they were not ready to do. I realized that a number of things needed to be in place and addressed **before** the client would feel safe enough to start the decluttering process.

Because the act of creating clutter can be defined as "decisions delayed" and making decisions takes brain power, decluttering can make people feel physically tired. Intense mental processes consume great amounts of glycogen in the brain. When glycogen is reduced, a person may feel disoriented This helps explain why so many people can feel dizzy while decluttering. If this happens to you, make sure to snack on healthy foods while working on lengthy decluttering projects.

The reduced glycogen, however, does not explain why so many people get emotional – sad, overwhelmed, angry – while clearing and organizing their spaces.

Every decluttering project is in fact a trip down memory lane, and down that path of remembrances we connect with the events and the emotions that we were experiencing at the time we purchased an object or received it as a gift. Other times, we will recover the memories and the feelings we had around the time we decided to put that object away or to stuff it somewhere, "out of sight, out of mind."

The decluttering process is a process of confronting many things about our lives that at some point we declined to confront. This takes courage, honesty, and **the will to be happy**. A healer I know told me recently, referring to a person who abandoned the treatment that was making them well, "the only incurable person is the one that refuses to confront life in full health." How true!

Decluttering is Step 7 in the Nine Steps to Feng Shui® Larger System

These days, I do not even address clutter with clients until the third session. My Nine Steps to Feng Shui® System is designed around three client visits, during which three steps of the program are addressed each time. Decluttering is, in my system, step 7, which shows you that there are six things you need to do to improve the Feng Shui of your home before you can be in a position to effectively and happily address decluttering.

The last page of this book has a listing of my other "Feng Shui Your Own..." series of books. I recommend that you check them out.

My Decluttering program, which is Step 7 of the larger Feng Shui program, **has itself nine steps.** I suggest you plan to progress on your decluttering journey by following the steps one by one. Their order is not random, it follows a **synergistic** method designed to help you achieve your clearing and organizing goals **with ease and grace.** Every step makes the next step a little easier.

Declutter Your Own Spaces

Step

1

The Right Amount of Storage

Making sure that you have the right amount of storage for the size of your home and the number of members in your family is essential to keeping a tidy home.

Sometimes messiness is simply a consequence of lack of storage. If a bedroom has a closet that is so small that a person has to wrestle with the hangers to get clothes in or out, it is likely that you will find clothes on the bed or on top of chairs in the bedroom.

STEP ONE: THE RIGHT AMOUNT OF STORAGE

Many times, clutter happens because there is simply not enough storage in a home.

Other times clutter happens because there is too much storage available.

1.1 Too Little Storage

When my husband and I moved to Iowa so that he could attend Palmer College of Chiropractic, we purchased a mobile home to keep our overhead low while he completed his studies.

Like most mobile homes and RVs, this one was a marvel of engineering when it came to storage. I have never before, or since, lived in a home that was so well designed in terms of meeting storage needs, compared to the square footage of the place.

The ample broom closet was big enough to accommodate a vacuum cleaner, brooms, mops, and the heavy coats that the Iowa winter required. Above the three-foot-by-three foot brooms closet there was a cabinet where the linens could be kept.

Likewise, the whole one side of the bedroom was occupied by a built in closet, with four smoothly sliding doors. My husband and I shared this closet with no problem, and never felt lacking in closet space.

The kitchen had plenty of high and low cabinets, of different depths. There was so much cabinet space that I never had to stack one pot inside the other.

When my spouse finished his studies and we moved to Tennessee and bought a "proper house" in a fairly new subdivision, we found that our new home was far from the smart design of our mobile home back in Iowa.

The brooms closet was **less than** two-by-two-feet. Once the vacuum cleaner went in, there was little room for anything else. There was a

Being able to make decisions is essential in the ability to continually create and recreate spaces where our authentic life can thrive.

1.3 The Right Amount of Storage

Architects have standards as to how much storage space a home needs to have. Building codes have standards way below that required for sensible architectural design. Builders abide by building codes, and not necessarily by the recommendations of architects. This means that unless you live in a high end home, custom designed by an architect, you probably lack storage space. Most homes under 2,000 square feet lack storage space.

Keep in mind that here we are talking about true needs for storage, that is, places to put away items that we use at least one time in every calendar year. We are not talking about perceived needs for storage that a person might have because they have trouble letting go of things.

On the next two pages you can see some summaries that I have put together regarding recommended storage for different needs in the home. These figures were arrived at by combining knowledge I acquired in the school of Architecture with Feng Shui knowledge and experience from working with numerous clients. Look at the suggestions and compare them with your needs and your experience, to make your own charts of needed storage space, then contrast this with the available storage in your home.

1.4 One Quarter Empty

For storage to be functional, you need to be able to move things around and to reach for the items you are looking for. Storage areas that are stuffed to the limit lose their functionality.

If you fill drawers all the way to the top, items tend to get stuck when opening and closing them. When kitchen cabinets are completely full, you can only see and access those items that are at the very front edge.

Learn to see storage areas as if they were three fourths of the actual volume. One fourth, or twenty five percent, needs to be left empty. This

When a cabinet is too full, you only have direct access to the items at the front, and it is not easy to keep track of its contents.

Minimum Required Storage (1)

CLOTHES

8 ft. of clothes closet width per person,
4 2-ft. wide drawers per person
+ 8 ft. for overflow per every four people in the home
COATS CLOSET: 2 ft. width per every person in the family.

BED LINENS

1 ft. of closet width per family member.

TOWELS

1 ft. of closet width per every two family members.

TABLE LINENS

1 2-ft. drawer or shelf for every family member.

Minimum Required Storage (2)

PAPERWORK

One file cabinet drawer per family member.

BOOKS

One 3-ft. wide, 5-shelves-high book shelf per person, ideally with doors you can close.

MEDIA

Mostly, CDs, DVDs, and Games
(sometimes, Audio and Video Cassettes or even LPs)
One 3ft. wide media organizer.

ORNAMENTS

The equivalent of one 2 ft. wide china cabinet for every two people in the home.

Minimum Required Storage (3)

FOOD
1 ft. width, 8 ft. tall pantry for every person in the home.

DISHWARE
One 2 ft. shelf/cabinet per person in the home,
4 drawers for utensils per family.

POTS AND PANS
Two 2 ft. shelves/cabinets per person in the home.

TOYS
Arts and crafts, hobbies, sports:
One 4′ x 2′ x2′ container per person.

Minimum Required Storage (4)

PERIODICALS
Newspapers: One 24″x12″x12″ box per family.
Magazines: One Magazine rack/shelf per family.
Newsletter/bulletins: One paper holder/tray per family.

MAIL
One in-box per person, one out-box per family.

MEDICINE CABINETS
1 per every two people.

BROOM CLOSET
One 3′ x 3′ closet per family.

HORIZONTAL SURFACE
Right inside and right outside of the entrance door
[to temporarily set things down].

STORAGE ROOM OR SHED
9 x 12′ or equivalent area in basement or attic.

twenty five percent allows for circulation within the space. Circulation is needed in small storage areas, such as drawers and cabinets, in the same way that it is needed in larger storage areas, such as attics – if you aren't able to walk into the attic, you won't be able to reach for any objects stored in this area, except for the ones closest to the door.

1.5 Fifteen Percent Storage

Architectural standards suggest devoting fifteen percent of the total area of a home to storage. This includes cabinets, closets, and storage rooms. However, I have found few homes that actually meet these standards.

One reason for this may be that built in storage places that require cabinetry are expensive and builders may avoid them to save money. Another reason may be that most people get more excited at the idea of larger living areas than the size of storage areas.

For example, for a home that is 2,000 sq. ft. you would need 300 sq. ft. devoted to storage. This is the equivalent of a 30 ft. x 10 ft. room. To give you an idea of what this means, in a starter home, children's bedrooms are around 10 x 10 ft., so we are talking about the area of three small bedrooms devoted to storage for a medium size home. Most homes do not have this much storage.

Is it any wonder that so many people end up using their garage for storage?

Make sure you have all the storage you need, but remember:

All storage areas must be 25% [1/4] empty, so you can find and remove things easily.

Total storage area in a home should be 15% or LESS [architectural standard]

1.6 Compensating for Lack of Storage

A remarkable example of a garage that doubles as tool shed and home gym. There is a place for everything and still room for the car.

Using the garage for storage is not in itself a problem. The problem comes when there is a conflict between one family member wishing to use the garage for storage while another family member wishes to put the car away in that area.

If a couple or a family decide to use the garage primarily for storage and organize it well, this can be a good solution for a home that offers too little storage space. After all, cars are designed to be outdoors, and in areas where crime is low and there is no vandalism, parking the car on the driveway is not a problem.

On the side bars of these pages I have placed some photos of one exceptional case where I found that the garage was being used for storage and as a tool shed and workshop, but was so well organized that you could also comfortable park two cars. If you take a careful look at these pictures, you may guess the secret of good storage: keep nothing on the floor that was not designed to go on the floor.

THE SECRET OF GOOD STORAGE IS:

NOTHING ON THE FLOOR...
that was not designed to be on the floor.
Every single item needs to have its place in a drawer, cabinet, shelf, hook or platform.

If after you have assessed your storage needs and compared them with what your home actually offers in terms of storage, and have concluded that you do not have enough storage space, then you can make some adjustments in terms of habits in order to cope with this.

Getting vacuum storage bags and putting away all the clothes that are not needed in the current season can multiply the space available in clothes closets and linen closets.

You can also streamline the contents of your clothes closets, to only keep the clothes that you love and use. Having fewer clothes may mean needing to do laundry more often. This is an example where housekeeping habits can help compensate for lack of storage.

Lack of storage can be replaced with habits and changes in lifestyle.

Renting a storage unit is another viable solution for lack of storage. The extra expense may be worth it in order to create more space for life at home.

Be careful when storing your things at the homes of friends or relatives. It is not a good idea to simply transfer your clutter to someone else's homes so you don't have to deal with it. Before you ever take a box to store at a loved one's home, go through it to make sure it contains things that you do want to keep, even though they don't need to be readily accessible.

Renting a storage unit can be a very good solution for a home with too little storage. However, make sure that you are not doing so just to avoid looking at your things and making the right decisions on what to do about your belongings.

Declutter Your Own Spaces

Step

60% Yang/40% Yin

A home without clutter and plenty of room for life is a balanced home, but balance is not 50/50. Human life thrives with a ratio of 3/2 Yang to Yin, in other words 60% Yang (Warm, Dry, Light) or Living Spaces and 40% Yin (Cool, Humid, Dark) for storage, circulation and cleaning spaces.

STEP TWO: 60% YANG / 40% YIN

In the previous chapter you learned how to figure out if you do not have enough storage space. But how about determining whether there is too much storage space in your home?

The answer is the balance of yin and yang.

2.1 The Forces of Yin and Yang

Opposites attract. The reason they attract is that they are trying to balance each other out: hot and cold; dark and light; narrow and wide; high and low; etc.

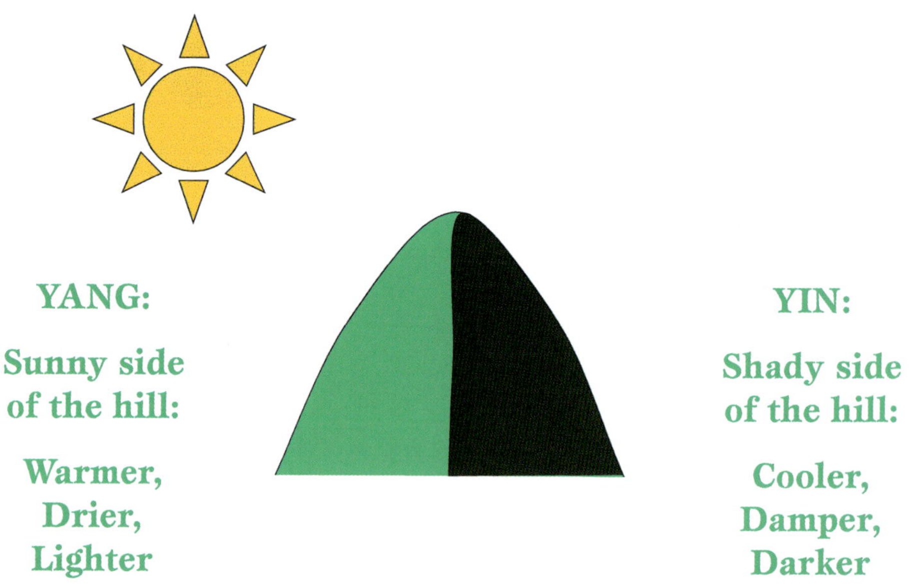

The sunny parts of the lot are yang, the shady parts of the lot are yin. People enjoy yang places with temporary or provisional shade the best. The yanger parts of your garden are the places that dry out first after the rain.

The most yin parts of your garden are those where the snow melts last.

Many people who grew up in Western culture misunderstand the concept of yin and yang as if it was a pendulum that always swings to one side and then to the other side with equal strength. The idea of yin and yang is a lot more complex.

If you take a look at the graphic of the Great Tai Chi, which is a term equivalent to the Universe, you will see that it symbolizes constant motion, where yin is constantly moving towards yang, and vice versa. You also will notice that the yang light portion contains a yin dot inside, and the yin dark portion contains a yang dot inside.

When yin reaches its maximum, it turns into yang; when yang reaches its maximum, it turns into yin.

We will explore the concept of yin and yang more when we look at the housekeeping waves in step 7.

Yin and Yang also determine the amount of space in a home that is devoted to active living space, versus the square footage devoted to storage and circulation.

2.2 The Ratio of Human Healthy Habitats

For yin and yang to be in balance in a home, they don't need to be on equal proportions of 50/50.

The ideal ratio for human health is of 3 of yang over 2 of yin, a 3:2 ratio, in other words 60% percent of yang and 40% of yin.

In a good architectural design, circulation areas – hallways, and staircases – need to occupy 25% or less of the surface. This makes an efficient design. Circulation areas are considered yin because the chi passes through them more quickly and does not settle, therefore it cannot concentrate enough for the area to become yang.

Storage areas are also yin because when people visit them they are usually in and out quickly, and do not perform activities there. Good architectural design requires 15% of storage space. Less than that, and the needs of the inhabitants are not covered, more than that increases the yin surface in a home and weakens the energy of the home.

You probably noticed that the 25% in circulation areas + the 15% in storage areas adds to 40%. However, notice that the recommendation is for circulation areas to occupy 25% or less of the total surface.

In Feng Shui we include bathrooms and laundry rooms in the list of yin areas.

The garage is also a yin area, however it is not considered towards the total count of square footage of yin space, because it was designed to house cars instead of people. Nevertheless, **a very unorganized garage can pull down the energy of the whole home.**

Homes with large unfinished attics and/or large unfinished basements run the risk of having an imbalance of yin and yang, where yin areas overpower the yang.

However, if an attic is well organized, it can be considered yang, because hot air goes up, and heat is yang. An unorganized attic would be counted as a yin space.

When it comes to unfinished basements, on the other hand, it doesn't matter if it is very organized. The unfinished basement is always considered yin.

If you find that the yin areas in your home occupy a larger surface than the yang areas, you need to take actions to balance the energy in your home.

Architectural standard:

Circulation areas should be 25% or less of the total area of a building.

Storage should be 15%.

This makes a building cost-efficient.

2.3 Yin and Yang Imbalances Generated by Unfinished Basements

If an unfinished basement is creating an imbalance of yin and yang , you may consider closing off a section of it, if doors are provided, or turning part of the area into a workshop room, if anyone in your home does handiwork. On the long term, you might consider making a plan to finish part of the basement.

2.4 Yin and Yang Imbalances Created by Junk Rooms

When there is an extra room in the home, it may originally be set up as a guest bedroom or a home office, but if it is not used often, there is always the temptation to start using it as a storage area. This is common for your couples and for empty-nesters as well.

Downsizing into a smaller home is, of course, an option, but not one that every person is prepared to choose.

I advise clients who are in this situation to connect with a passion, something they want to do, for which they could use the space.

Keeping a computer or workout equipment in a master bedroom is very negative for the relationship and counterproductive for deep rest, so it is an excellent idea to take these items away from the master bedroom and place them in another room that is vacant or that has been turned into a junk room.

Other clients may want to go back to a hobby that was given up many years ago.

Often, a good idea is to turn the room into a reading, meditation and yoga room.

The color yellow can be helpful in counteracting the excessive yin of an unfinished basement.

2.5 Compensating for Too Much Yin

There will be cases when the yin areas are greater than the yang areas and none of the above solutions apply.

For example, you may have an unfinished basement that is as large as the main floor in the home, and not have any means to finish or close off part of it.

In cases like these, you can increase the yang in the yin space by adding the color yellow, and objects that are bright and colorful, especially artwork on the walls, or even a bright mural.

It is also a good idea to have very good lighting in an unfinished basement. The areas can be scary for children, but with bright lights feelings of fear will be diminished.

Yang Areas [60% or more]

Kitchen

Dining Room

Family Room

Living Room

Bedrooms

Foyer

Yin Areas [40% or less]

Bathrooms

Laundry

Storage

Basements (unfinished)

Junk rooms

Hallways, staircases

Declutter Your Own Spaces

Step

Open Up Circulation

Free up circulation in entries, hallways and staircases, and underneath furniture.

Wherever there is life there is chi. Even though most people cannot see chi, we all can recognize the presence of life.

STEP THREE: OPEN UP CIRCULATION

Chi is a Chinese term translated as "Life Force." Most people cannot see chi but most can be trained to feel it in their hands in less than one minute.

If you have ever done yoga, tai chi, or belly dancing you probably have felt a warm, tingling, magnetic sensation in your fingertips. You were perceiving chi, the life force.

To better understand chi we compare it to things we know, like the wind, water flowing, light, sound and children.

• Beneficial chi moves in a slow meandering way, like a soft breeze.

• Chi can stagnate, like water, if it stops moving. When chi flowing alongside two walls meets at the corner, it creates turbulence, like when two rivers meet.

• Chi is a more subtle energy than light, so anything that produces an effect on light also produces an effect on chi.

• Chi is absorbed by porous surfaces and bounces off smooth surfaces, like sound.

THERE ARE THREE KINDS OF CHI

Beneficial chi, slow moving and meandering

Destructive or cutting chi, due to excessive speed, winding motion or turbulence

Stagnant chi, due to lack of movement

• Chi is attracted by anything that would attract a toddler, and is sent away by anything that would scare a toddler.

There are three main principles of Chi:

- Where there is Life there is Chi
- Chi connects everything
- Chi is in constant motion, producing changes as it moves

3.1 Three Kinds of Chi

Beneficial chi - bright, meandering chi.

Cutting chi - chi that moves too fast.

Stagnant chi - not enough chi or decayed chi.

Clutter promotes
STAGNANT CHI
and does not allow
beneficial chi to circulate.

In Feng Shui terms, this is not conducive to a healthy home.

Definition of clutter:

a confused multitude of things.

My Definition of Clutter:

Decisions Delayed.

3.2 What to Do to Have Healthy Chi

In order to achieve a healthy circulation of the Life Force you need to:

1 Invite and collect beneficial chi

2 Slow down/ disperse destructive chi

3 Stir up stagnant chi, prevent chi drainage

My book *Feng Shui Your Own Home* describes how to address items 1 and 2. This book, which specializes in decluttering, deals with item 3, how to prevent the stagnation of chi.

3.3 Stagnant Chi In Corners

Stagnant chi occurs when there is no chi movement and there is a **loss of vitality** in the space. However, not all clutter has the same severity in Feng Shui. This chapter deals with the most destructive clutter in a home.

Stagnant chi is frequently found in the inside of corners where walls meet. These corners are like a magnet for clutter, unless they are occupied by a piece of furniture, a plant or a light source.

You can also activate the chi in corners with a mobile or a crystal hanging from the ceiling. If you do not give a specific use to corners, they become places where people always feel tempted to place things, that do not belong there.

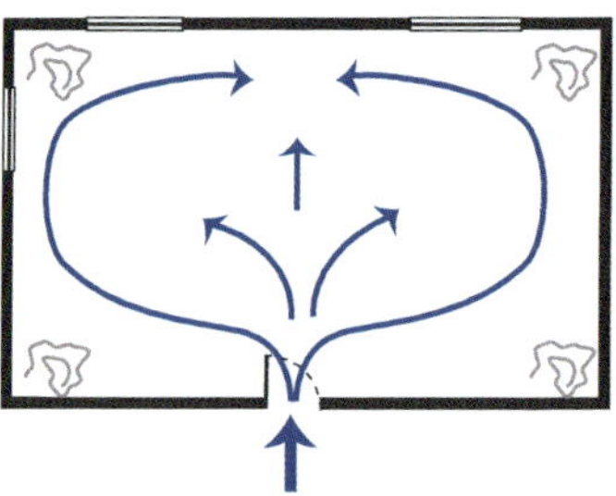
Chi gets stagnated in corners.

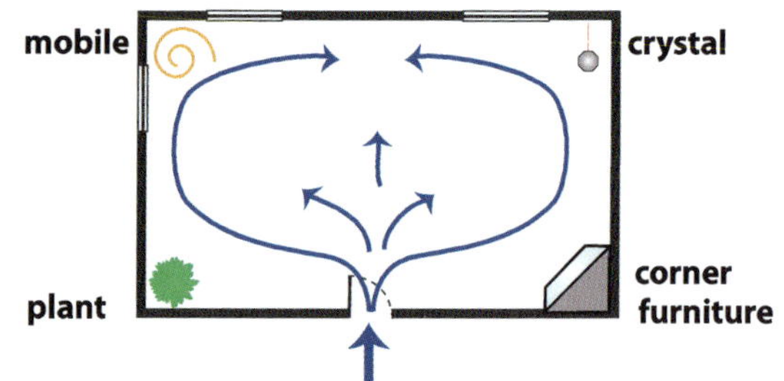

Cure the corners of every room.

3.3 No Clutter by the Entrance - Outside

Comedian Jeff Foxworthy has a joke that says, "If people stop by your house every day thinking you are having a yard sale – you might be a red-neck."

The type of clutter that is most damaging to your **reputation** is any kind of clutter located between the curb and the main door.

I have seen many beautiful, ideal Feng Shui entrances from the design view point, ruined by the addition of clutter.

Take a look at your main entrance: what is around it? Are there any items by the main door that do not belong there?

If you have a porch: is there any furniture that has outlived its usefulness? Are there any items you do not love, or that bring you bad memories? Remove them and you will see how much more uplifted you will feel when you come home.

THE IDEAL ENTRANCE

This graphic describes what you need to have a good Feng Shui entrance. If you have a porch by the main entrance, then having seating or even a table and chairs would be good, but never use your porch for storage!

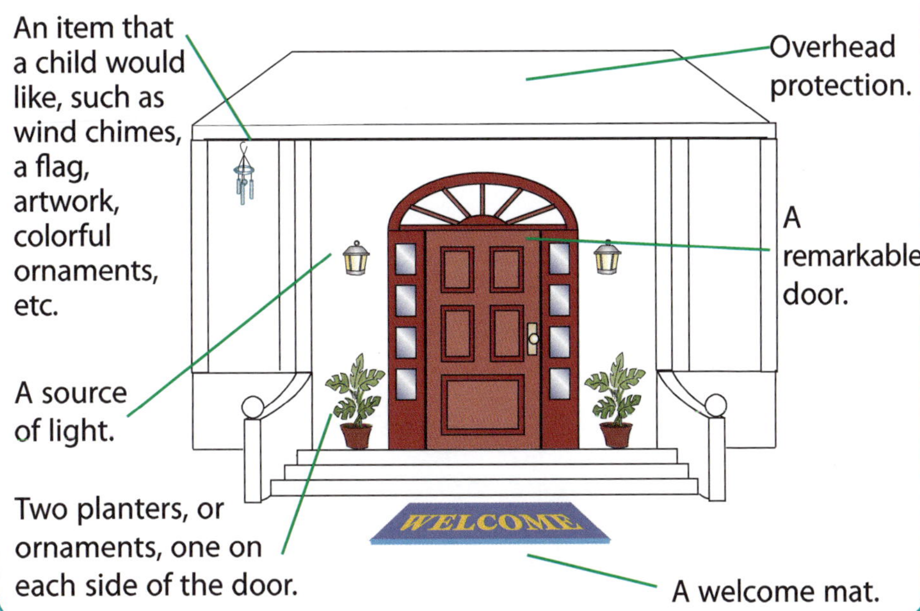

Choosing the Main Entrance

The front door is the main entrance in most cases. If you use another door a lot more often than the front door, answer these questions:

1. Where do you get your mail?
2. Where do private delivery services drop off packages?
3. If you had guests that were very important to you, which door would you have them use?

If the answer to any of the above questions is "the front door" then you should consider this your main door, even if you mostly use another door.

If you NEVER use your front door, then your side/back/garage door [the one you use the most] should be considered your main door.

Exception: Never assign a back door accessed from an alley as a main door if there is a slope going up from the road to the front door of the house.

Do not use the space behind doors as storage. Doors should open fully, to 90° or 180°

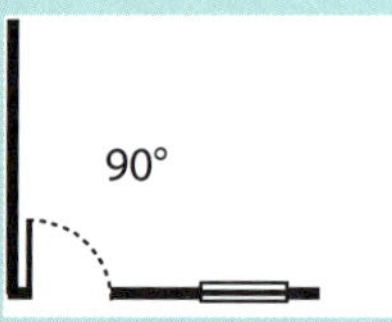

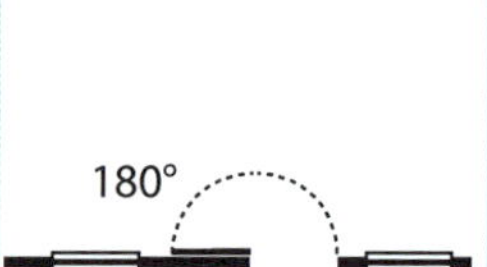

[this is even more important for the entrance doors]

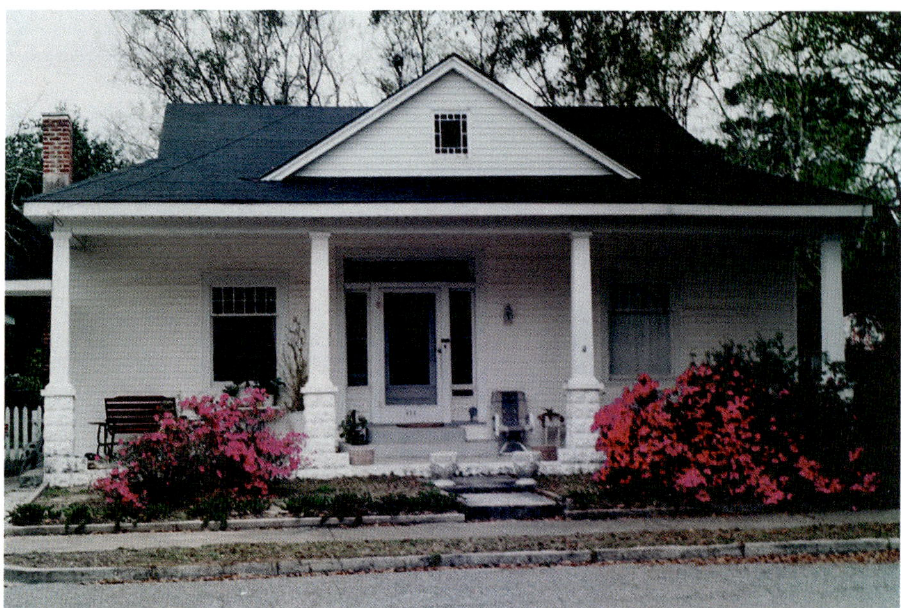

Arrange large porches as outside sitting or visiting areas, or fill them up with plants. If you use your front porch as a storage area, even if it is to place items there temporarily as a staging place before you take them to a thrift shop, this affects negatively how other people perceive you.

3.4 No Clutter by the Entrance - Inside

The main entrance is considered the "mouth of chi," the door that allows the life force to come into the home in larger amounts than any other door in the home.

If the "mouth of chi" is obstructed, the vitality of the whole home with be affected and reduced. A home with low vitality is a home that in Feng Shui is believed to cause the inhabitants to feel lacking in energy. Lack in energy translates into poor motivation for house-keeping, and poor housekeeping is likely to result in more clutter and stagnation, making it ever more difficult to clean up and organize.

What you see when you first come into the home determines how you perceive the whole home and your life. Make sure you see something beautiful and uplifting. If the first thing you see is clutter, then you are giving yourself bad feedback about your life.

The most important place in the home to keep clear of clutter is the space behind the main door. The door must open without obstructions to the full extent allowed by the location of walls, either 90° or 180°, as you can see in the graphic below.

3.5 No Clutter In Hallways or Staircases

The second most important spaces in the home to keep free of clutter are hallways and staircases, especially those closest to the entrance doors.

In addition to issues with clutter and stagnation, any objects placed in hallways or staircases constitute a threat to safety.

Only place artwork or mirrors in narrow hallways. Mirrors and artwork with long distance perspective are desired on the side walls of hallways, and bright, colorful artwork with large images is desired at the end of hallways.

You may place tables that are not very deep, eighteen inches or less, if the hallways is **at least** four feet wide. Half moon tables are preferred or rectangular tables with rounded corners.

Only artwork is allowed on the walls to the sides of, or alongside, staircases. The steps themselves need to be kept completely clear of everything. NOTHING should go on the steps that was not designed to go specifically on the steps.

When it comes to staircases safety comes first!

Do not decorate staircase steps. Steps need to be completely clear of anything that was not designed to go on them.

For example, you can place a well secured runner on the steps, or thin mats or decorations designed that are fixed to the steps to prevent sliding.

However, do not attempt to decorate the steps themselves with any ornaments, because they will just become hazards.

Decorate the walls with small, light paintings or prints.

Do not place furniture in hallways if they are less than 4 ft. wide.

In hallways wider than 4 ft. and that are close to the main entrance, place a half-moon welcome table that is not very deep.

It is much easier to convince a child that there are no monsters under the bed if you can demonstrate there is nothing under the bed.

3.6 No Clutter Underneath Furniture

It is very inauspicious to keep clutter under furniture, but it is especially bad to keep clutter under beds.

For starters, whenever objects are left underneath the bed, that space gets cleaned a lot less often than if the space is clear. When people are sleeping, the free flow of chi under the beds guarantees better rest and repair of mind and body. Having stagnation under the bed is very negative. This doesn't only apply to objects thrown in the floor carelessly and then kicked under the bed, but also to storage containers that were designed to go under the bed.

Many people tend to stuff items that don't actually have a place in the home underneath furniture. For people with tendencies to clutter, clear space is translated as "space available" for stuffing things into.

Live by this rule: **keep nothing on the floor that was not designed to be on the floor,** especially underneath pieces of furniture. Living by this rule makes cleaning a lot easier and guarantees a better circulation of chi.

In Feng Shui terms, having "stuff" underneath furniture impedes the circulation of beneficial chi, while at the same time creating stagnant [dead] chi.

Reasons why it is a bad idea to have anything under furniture [even storage containers designed to go there]:

- You clean less.
- Less cleaning means dust accumulates.
- Dust is over 70% dead skin cells from people and animals.
- Dead cells attract dust mites and other allergens.

Declutter Your Own Spaces

Step

Work with the Natural Rhythms

At any time we can choose whether to go with nature or against it.

We tend to do a lot better when we tune in to the rhythms, movements and energies of nature.

All clocks and calendars should show the right time and the right date.

An antique clock may be very beautiful, but if it does not show the right time, it is bad Feng Shui.

Invitations and greeting cards can become a source of clutter.

STEP FOUR: WORK WITH THE NATURAL RHYTHMS

There is a basic rhythm in all of Creation that is expressed in the movement of our planet as well as in our breathing. The seasons of the year, the hours in a day, the phases of the moon, all revolve around this basic pattern. When we live by that rhythm we tend to do better.

This basic rhythm has four energetic movements:

- **Rising** energy: spring / dawn and morning / crescent moon / inhaling / East
- **Radiating** energy: summer / Midday / full moon / full lung expansion / South (Northern Hemisphere) or North (Southern Hemisphere)
- **Descending** energy: fall / afternoon and sunset / waning moon/ exhaling / West
- **Halting** energy: winter / 12 midnight / new moon / emptying of the lungs in preparation for the next breathing cycle / North (Northern Hemisphere) or South (Southern Hemisphere)

4.1 Time and Timing - Calendars and Clocks

In order for us to be able to take advantage of opportunities we need to be at the right place at the right time, and for us to do this it is necessary that we become aware of the current time.

To show the Universe you are lined up with the current energies of time and timing, all clocks must be in good working condition and show the right time, and all calendars must show the right day, week or month.

Clocks and calendars that do not show the current date and time create an element of distrust within the home. For example, if you are getting ready to go and need to check the time, your mind directs you to the nearest clock. When you look up (or down) at it, if the clock has recently stopped and you are not aware that it is showing an incorrect time, you might be early or late to wherever you need to go. However if the clock has stopped working for a while, almost as soon as you see it, you will remember that you cannot go by what it says *you cannot trust it*. Much peace of mind can be added to a home by making sure that all clocks, watches and calendars are set to reflect true dates and times.

I have been to homes where there wasn't a single clock showing the right time, and to homes where clocks had been broken for years and never fixed. These are considered inauspicious in Feng Shui. In general, you shouldn't keep any objects in the home that are not functioning. You either make a plan to fix them, or simply let them go.

Calendars of years past are a source of paper clutter in many homes. Sometimes people hold on to them because they are very fond of the images. If this is your case, you can cut out the photo or image you like and put it in a pretty frame, or keep it in a binder where you collect beautiful images.

Other times, we may feel attachment to the notes that we made on a calendar, because it feels like a journal of sorts. In this case, I suggest you place old calendars in the Blessings Bag or Box described on the side bar.

4.2 Invitations and Cards

Another common source of clutter in homes is created by invitations to events that already happened, and by greeting cards.

There are often strong emotions associated with letting go of invitations and cards because they bring memories of events or kind gestures from others.

Even though we know that there is no longer a use for them, it feels wrong to simply put them in the trash.

However, it also feels wrong when a drawer gets stuck because it is filled with these cards.

I recommend that you use a system that is somewhere in between recycling them right away and keeping them for years.

Set aside a beautiful bag or box and place all expired invitations and

Blessings Bag

Choose a very pretty bag (or box) to use as a "blessings bag" – a container used to keep invitations for events that have already happened and greeting cards after the holiday or special occasion has passed.

This is a temporary home for these items so that they do not create clutter in drawers, counter tops and refrigerator doors.

When the bag is full, or according to a schedule you have set, take the contents to a recycling site and let them go.

You may say a prayer before doing so, declaring to the Universe that you accept and keep the love and the relationships, and you are only letting go of the paper.

Of course, do not let go of any invitations or greeting cards that are very significant to you and that you would like to keep as mementos. In this case, place them in a photo album or scrapbook.

Help Nature Too!

Choose cleaning products that are gentle to the environment, to your spaces, and to your health.

Today there are several brands of products that clean very efficiently with natural blends, which do not pollute nature.

greeting cards in them. You may also include any other pieces of paper that remind you of fond times, such as tickets to a concert or a play. Set up a rhythm by which to let go of these items. This rhythm will depend on how large the bag or box is, and how busy your social life is. You may choose to empty it out every quarter, twice a year, or once a year.

Place all old invitations and greeting cards in the bag or box as soon as the event you were invited to has happened, and no more than a week or two after the event for which you received a greeting card has passed. When you are ready, per your chosen rhythm, take the contents of the bag or box to the recycling collection site or put them in the recycling container in your home if you get curb side recycling collection. Before you put them in though, say a prayer or a statement along these lines:

"I am grateful for the relationships and the good wishes. I keep the love, and only let go of the paper."

"I am grateful for the relationships and the good wishes. I keep the love, and let go of the paper."

4.3 Let Nature Help You Clear Spaces

In times past it was common to have housekeeping routines that helped keep chi healthy inside a home. Even though the concept of chi might have been foreign to the house keepers of the past, they had a sense that air circulation and sunshine were important to keep a home in good condition.

Habits like opening up curtains or blinds first thing in the morning and cracking the windows open even for just a few minutes every day have seemingly become unnecessary with the advent of electricity and central air and heating. However, in terms of chi, these habits are still needed to keep the circulation of the life force at healthy levels in the home.

In order to be able to access windows to open up window treatments and the windows themselves, it is necessary to have unrestricted access to windows.

Never block windows with furniture. Avoid placing heavy or bulky pieces of furniture in front of windows, even if they do not block the light. Being able to reach windows for opening is also a safety issue, to use as an exit in case of an emergency. Make sure that every space in your home has at least one window that opens fully, easily and smoothly.

Sunshine has healing properties and is a source of life. In the winter, open up window treatments during the hours of the day that sunshine comes in.

You can use mirrors to double the time that the sunshine comes in. Never place a magnifying mirror near a window where you get sunshine, as this could be a cause of fire.

Even in the middle of the summer and the winter months make sure that you open up two outside doors at the same time at least two or three times per week, ideally every day, for a minimum of five minutes.

During the Spring and Fall, open windows and doors whenever it is convenient. You will save money in electricity and have cleaner air inside the home. Outside air has negative ions, which are good for us despite their name, and is charged by sunshine – let it in.

Let the sun and the air do part of the work for you:

- **The sun disinfects and bleaches, it also gets rid of stagnant chi, and impregnates things with beneficial chi. Become a "sun chaser" especially in the winter.**
- **Make sure all the doors and windows in the building open and close smoothly, so you can easily invite breezes in.**
- **Never block doors or windows and avoid blocking the access to windows [so they can be opened].**

Opening up curtains and other window treatments allows natural light in.

It is very important to keep in touch with the outside world.

Make sure that you can access easily and freely at least one window in every space.

Windows should open easily and completely.

Areca Palm

Money Plant

Snake Plant

4.4 Cleaning Inside Air

Air that is re-circulated within a building becomes stale. You also need to be aware that there are many sources of indoor pollution, either coming from building materials, paints, floor lacquers, but also from furniture.

Some common indoor pollutants are: tobacco smoke, formaldehyde, lead, pesticides, and asbestos.

Air filters and purifiers are good additions to the home. Ionic filters and fans can also help improve the air and chi quality indoors.

4.5 Plants that Clean Inside Air

Certain plants can help create clean indoor air. There are some projects in India, that were tried in areas with heavy air pollution, where the air inside buildings became a lot healthier than outside air by the use of large numbers of these plants. In these studies they found that people suffering from respiratory ailments due to the bad quality of air in the city quickly improved.

NASA has also done experiments on air quality improvement with the use of plants.

I have listed several plants here, but have omitted other plants that even though they help clean the air, are not Feng-Shui correct due to the shape of their leaves, or because they are spiky.

4.5.1 Peace Lily (Spathiphyllum)

This plant helps clean the air of benzene, a carcinogen found in paints and varnishes. It is also effective in removing acetone, that can be emitted by electronic equipment, adhesives and some household cleaners.

4.5.2 Snake Plant (Sansevieria trifasciata)

Also known as mother-in-law's tongue. It absorbs carbon dioxide and releases oxygen during the night, whereas most other plants release oxygen only during the day. It also removes formaldehyde and benzene from the air. This is one plant that is considered Feng Shui correct for bedrooms.

4.5.3 Money Plant (Epipremnum aureum)

This vine helps remove formaldehyde, carbon monoxide and benzene. This is a good plant to keep in garages or near entrances that connect the home with the garage, to help deal with the fumes.

4.5.4 Areca Palm (Chrysalidocarpus lutescens)

This plant absorbs formaldehyde, benzene, carbon monoxide, xylene, and chloroform. It also emits moisture, so it is helpful in dry areas or during the winter.

4.5.5 Mums (Chrysanthemum)

This plant removes benzene from the air. Benzene is one of the most common odorless pollutants found in inks, paints, plastic, dyes, detergents, gasoline, pharmaceuticals, and pesticides.

4.6 Decluttering by Seasons

Decluttering the home is akin to cleansing the body. There are two seasons when cleansing and decluttering become easier, as nature is helping the processes.

These two seasons are the Spring and Fall. However, this does not mean that decluttering projects should not be started in the Summer and Winter. It means that it is better to embark on certain decluttering projects according to the season that makes it easier to declutter that particular aspect.

Larger decluttering projects, especially those that require being outdoors or going back and forth from the inside to the outside are better done in the Spring and Fall.

Smaller projects, especially those that can be done indoors are better for the Summer and Winter, of course this is provided that your home is air conditioned in the Summer. The relationship between the types of clutter and the Feng Shui life areas also influence the recommendations on what to declutter in which season.

Chrysanthemum

Peace Lily

Plants in Bedrooms

The Feng Shui rule is **no plants in bedrooms.** Exceptions are the Snake Plant, a few orchids, and bromeliads, which release oxygen at night. Most plants only release oxygen during the day.

4.6.1 Spring

The Spring is associated with the life areas that have to do with growth and upward movement, these are the ones related to health and wealth. Because of these associations, it is a good idea to declutter and organize clothes closet and drawers, pantries and gardening sheds.

4.6.2 Summer

The Summer is connected with all the objects associated with social life – movies, music CDs, entertainment centers and ornaments placed in the family room.

4.6.3 Fall

The season of Fall is related to the objects in the home that have to do with children, handiwork, fun and creativity. Declutter toys, play and game rooms, art and hobby rooms, and tool sheds.

4.6.4 Winter

The Winter is the time of the year when we evaluate the past and make plans for the future. It is a good time to deal with paper work. Declutter book shelves, filing cabinets, and any kitchen drawers where you keep papers.

What to Declutter and Organize...

In the Spring **CLOTHES CLOSETS AND DRAWERS, PANTRIES AND GARDENING SHEDS**	**In the Summer** **ENTERTAINMENT CENTERS, DRESSERS, CURIO CABINETS**
In the Fall **TOY CHESTS, TOOL SHEDS, COUNTERS AND SHELVES**	**In the Winter** **BOOKSHELVES, FILING CABINETS, KITCHEN DRAWERS**

4.7 Housekeeping Processes

Housework may seem never ending, but it helps to think that every aspect, every action that forms part of house keeping, does have a beginning and an end.

This section is not intended to be a manual on housework or to give all the answers on developing good housekeeping habits. There are very good books on the subject. These are just some suggestions on how people with very tight schedules – and not particularly inclined to house chores – might tackle them in more efficient and less tiresome ways.

The desire to keep a space **always** tidy and spotless is perhaps the straightest path to a messy place.

The many acts involved in living and working demand that things get taken out of their places, that they get used, worn and made dirty. We need to learn to accept these facts and deal with them as the moments and rhythms of our lives allow and require.

Many people get frustrated at the never-ending nature of housekeeping chores. They say they do not mind housework per-se, but rather the monotony of having to do things over and over again. If you feel like this, it may help to consider that just like the succession of day and night is never-ending but every single day does have a beginning and an end, so does every cycle of house cleaning and organizing.

There is a process by which things get disorganized and dirty. Find processes to reverse this direction and go back to a state of cleanliness and order.

What follows are some practices that may help you make your housekeeping processes easier.

4.7.1 Simultaneity

With the aid of machines, many house chores that do not depend on or follow each other can be performed simultaneously. We can be doing laundry while vacuuming and while cooking a pot of beans. Of course, at any particular moment your attention will be devoted to just one of them. We do need to mind the vacuum cleaner whenever it is on, but you do not have to watch over the washer and dryer or stand constantly by the pot. Water, electricity and fire get these things done for us.

In modern society, devices and appliances make house keeping much easier – they multiply our time and lessen our load.

Multiply your time by performing two non-related house chores simultaneously, when technology allows it.

Doing laundry is a perfect match for dusting and vacuuming. While cooking or baking, you can clean up kitchen counters. If you have a dishwasher, mop the kitchen floor while you do the dishes.

It doesn't work as well to plan to do something "fun" while waiting for a machine to be done because of the different kind of energy required and the mindset related to working as opposed to having fun. For example, if we choose to watch a movie while doing laundry, it becomes a nuisance to have to pause it to go check on the machine and/or continue with the chore, or we even might forget about it altogether. The one exception is that of listening to music and to audio-books, which you can do while performing mechanical housekeeping activities. The latter are especially helpful if you enjoy reading but have a hard time finding time to do it.

4.7.2 Synchronizing

Make the most out of your time by synchronizing related cycles.

Say for example that you want to boil some broccoli florets. Washing and cutting the vegetables, then putting on a pot of water to boil is not as efficient as having the pot with water up on the stove before you wash and cut the vegetables, so that by the time you are finished cutting them, the water is already boiling. Synchronizing is especially important in the kitchen but it also applies to other areas of the house. Find out how much time the washer takes to complete different washing cycles in different size loads. Do the same for the drying cycles of your dryer, so that you can be sure to complete the cycle – including folding and hanging clothes so that they won't wrinkle – before going to bed or going out.

Mop after sweeping and when you know you have enough time to let the floor dry.

Make the most out of your time by synchronizing related cycles.

4.7.3 Get the Right Tools

When buying cleaning tools, make sure what you choose will get the job done. There is no value in saving money to buy a device you will not use because it is uncomfortable, or that will make you do things twice because once wasn't enough.

Get commercial and industrial quality tools, accessories and devices. The extra cost will end up saving you money over the years, and they will make your chores much easier. Pay special attention to the quality of:

- Vacuum cleaners
- Trash cans
- Dusters
- Mops
- Cooking Pots
- Garden Tools

Get commercial and industrial quality tools, accessories and devices.

1. **Whenever possible, perform non-successive cycles simultaneously.**
2. **Synchronize related cycles.**
3. **Get the right tools.**

Where dust collects, chi stagnates.

For some housework chores, it really pays to invest in equipment that is commercial or industrial quality.

Close any cycle you have started before the beginning of the same one or the next related cycle.

4.8 House Keeping Rhythms

Completing or "Closing" cycles

A **cycle** is a complete set of events that keep coming back in the same order, and usually take a constant period of time.

A cycle can be represented in the graphic of a wave. The generic house keeping wave looks like this:

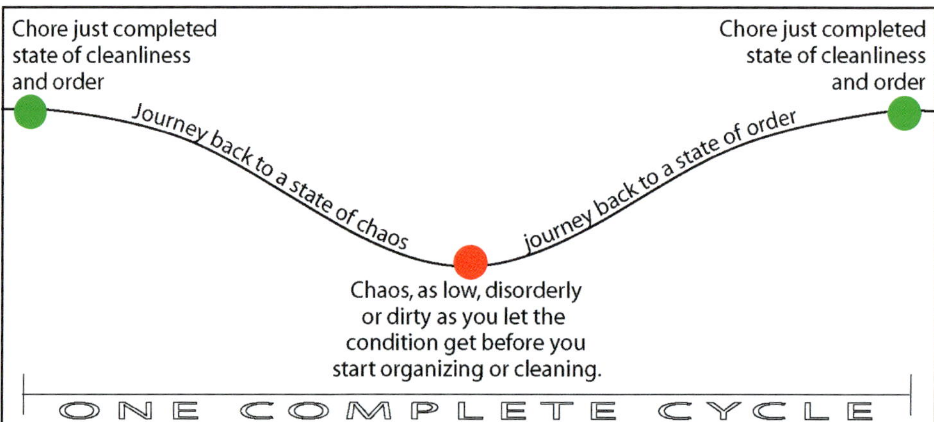

Obviously, one complete cycle takes a certain amount of time. The speed at which the cycle of a chore is completed determines the frequency at which it is performed. People whose homes or offices appear to be always tidy are probably just cleaning and organizing at a higher frequency – that is, more frequently than others, but we all have to deal with chaos, there is no way to avoid it, as it is part of life.

For example, one Saturday morning a family leaves their kitchen very clean and organized, then they go grocery shopping. When they come back, they will set down bags and boxes all over the kitchen. This is the state of chaos. Then they will put away every item they bought and the kitchen will go back to a state of order. The grocery shopping cycle is closely related to the cycles of filling up and then gradually emptying out refrigerators and pantries.

Properly completing, or "closing" cycles that we have started is the key to a tidy space.

Check the charts in the next two pages for a reference on how different kinds of housekeeping waves would affect the way in which the cleanliness and orderliness of a place are perceived.

When one cycle is not completed before the same or a related cycle starts over, then we invite chaos to be the **prevalent** state of our space. For example, when we start cooking while there are still pots and dishes in the sink from the previous meal.

Many times, it may be better not to start a cycle if we know that we do not have the time to finish it up before the next related cycle is to begin. For example, dirty pots and dishes being soaked in the sink will not interfere with your "doing laundry" cycle. However, if you decide to do your laundry and find that someone else has a recently washed load still in the washing machine, while they have not removed a previous load from the dryer either, this will certainly interrupt the flow of your planned chore.

Keep in mind that a generic cycle like "cleaning and disinfecting the bathroom" can be subdivided into smaller and shorter cycles like cleaning the tub, the shower, the toilet, the sink, the vanity mirror, the floor – each one of these can be done at separate instances if your schedule does not allow you to clean the whole bathroom at one time, or if you are not inclined to do it.

Some large housekeeping tasks can be subdivided into smaller, shorter activities, than can be performed at different times.

By breaking up activities and closing every cycle you may incorporate a sense of achievement and completion into your housekeeping chores.

Some cycles like dish washing, are repeated several times in a day, others once a day, once every other day, twice a week, once a week, once a month, every quarter, once a year, etc. If housekeeping does not come naturally to you, it might help to write up a schedule of activities and their frequencies.

By breaking up activities and closing every cycle you may incorporate a sense of achievement and completion into your housekeeping chores.

WE ARE ALL TIDY

The standards for cleanliness and order are not equal for all people. The same is true for the degree of disorder and "dirtiness" that a person can tolerate.

For some people, for example, the signal that it is time to do the dishes is seeing one dirty fork in the sink. For others it is having a sink full of soapy water and dishes. Yet for others it may be two sinks overflowing with dirty dishes and pots, or enough items to fill up the dishwasher. And some others may feel it is time to do the dishes when they run out of clean dishware... or when they run out of disposable ware... or when they run out of money to buy more disposable ware. Of course there are lots of points in-between all of the mentioned examples. The bottom line is that we all have a bottom line of untidiness, at which time we start to clean and organize.

Continuing this example of doing dishes, for some people this cycle is only complete when the dishes have been washed, dried, and put away in cupboards. Others will only consider they are done after wiping the dining table, the kitchen counters and the stove or microwave. Yet for others it ends when the clean dishes and pots are set on a wire container to drain the water. For others it may end when they have washed just

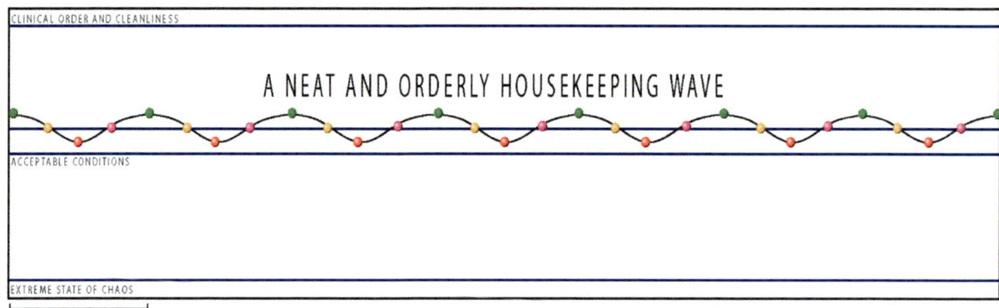

ONE COMPLETE CYCLE

The blue line indicates the average perception of the space as tidy or untidy

- Chore just completed - the state of cleanliness and order with which you feel comfortble
- Journey back to a state of chaos, a natural consequence of living
- Chaos, as low, disorderly or dirty as you let the condition get before you start organizing or cleaning.
- Performing the housework, the road back to a state of order

As you can see in the chart above, the key to a place that gives the general appearance of tidiness is to set your personal "state of chaos" right above the line indicating "Acceptable Conditions" - Notice that there is continuity and a rythm established by the routines of housekeeping.

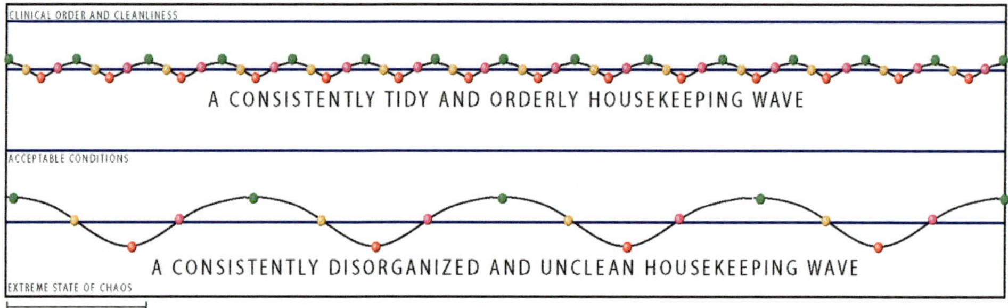

ONE COMPLETE CYCLE

The blue line indicates the average perception of the space as tidy or untidy

- Chore just completed - the state of cleanliness and order with which you feel comfortble
- Journey back to a state of chaos, a natural consequence of living
- Chaos, as low, disorderly or dirty as you let the condition get before you start organizing or cleaning.
- Performing the housework, the road back to a state of order

A tidy and neat person probably maintains a housekeeping wave like the one on top. Notice that the frequency (number of complete cycles in a period of time) is increased and that the amplitude (the vertical distance between the green dot and the red dot) is decreased.

When a space is perceived as sloppy, it probably means that the frequency of housechores has decreased and that the amplitude has increased. Notice that there is still a consistent and rythmical approach to housekeeping, but because the standards were set relatively low, the general appearance may be that of despondency.

CLINICAL ORDER AND CLEANLINESS

OUTSIDE OF A CLINICAL ENVIRONMENT,THIS KIND OF HOUSEKEEPING EVOKES AN OBSESIVE CUMPULSIVE BEHAVIOR, DISORDER IS A BY-PRODUCT OF LIVING, IT NEEDS TO BE DEALTH WITH, NOT ELIMINATED TO THE POINT WHERE WE CANNOT ENJOY LIFE.

ACCEPTABLE CONDITIONS

THE WAVE OF APATHY - NOT CARING ANY MORE

EXTREME STATE OF CHAOS

ONE COMPLETE CYCLE

The blue line indicates the average perception of the space as tidy or untidy

- Chore just completed - the state of cleanliness and order with which you feel comfortble
- Journey back to a state of chaos, a natural consequence of living
- Chaos, as low, disorderly or dirty as you let the condition get before you start organizing or cleaning.
- Performing the housework, the road back to a state of order

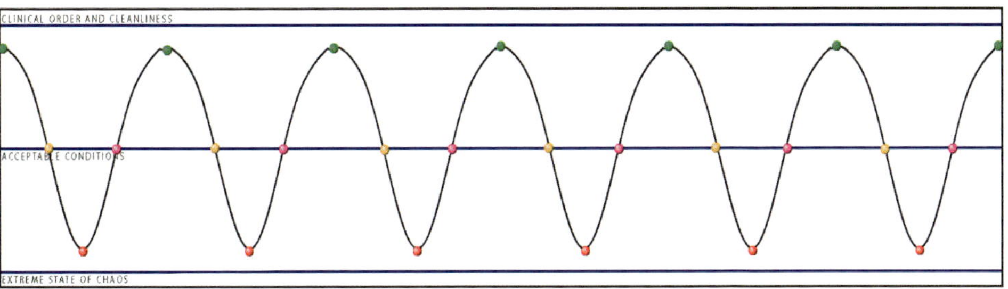

ONE COMPLETE CYCLE

The blue line indicates the average perception of the space as tidy or untidy

- Chore just completed - the state of cleanliness and order with which you feel comfortble
- Journey back to a state of chaos, a natural consequence of living
- Chaos, as low, disorderly or dirty as you let the condition get before you start organizing or cleaning.
- Performing the housework, the road back to a state of order

THIS KIND OF CURVE WILL WEAR YOU OUT! ...AND YOUR SPACE WILL STILL NOT GIVE AN APPEARANCE OF TIDINESS, JUST BARELY ACCEPTABLE IT ALSO EVOKES MANIC-DEPRESSIVE BEHAVIORS... SOMETIMES REAL HIGH, SOMETIMES REAL LOW

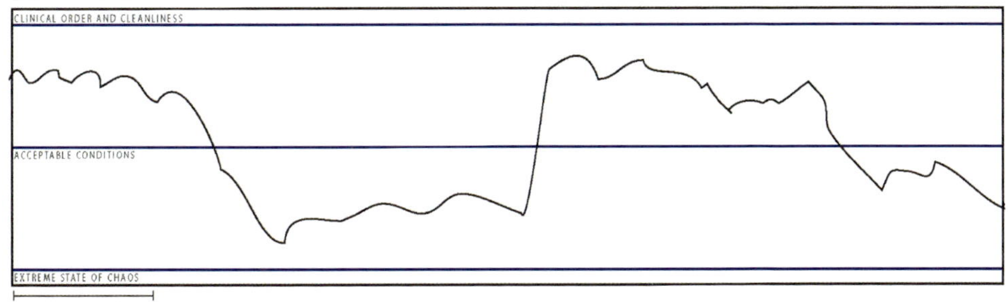

ONE COMPLETE CYCLE

The blue line indicates the average perception of the space as tidy or untidy

A TOTALLY CAOTHIC CURVE, WITH NO RYTHM AND NO SET STANDARDS WILL STRESS YOU OUT UNECESSARILY!

enough pots and dishes to get by the next meal.

In the graphics on these two pages the green dots represent various standards of order and cleanliness, while the red dots represent the signal to start doing housework. Both are subjective, but depending on how high standards are set our places will give a general appearance of order or disorder.

We are all tidy, as we all clean up and organize some, but the question is: Does our place look tidy for the general observer? If it doesn't and we would like it to give a message of cleanliness and order, we need to raise our standards, which can be easily done by increasing the frequency at which we tidy up and having an organizing system, so that we do not have to create unnecessary disorder. (For example, if we know where a piece of clothing is, we do not need to extract the whole contents of a drawer to find it).

Instead of letting the place go until reaching your red signal, catch the flow halfway, where the yellow dot is, and make that your new red dot. See the figure at the top of the next page.

Housekeeping depends on habits. Habits are behaviors learned by the body, not the mind. Changing habits starts with a decision of the mind, which is very quick, but habits can only be acquired with gradual retraining of the body.

Re-define yourself as a person who loves house work.

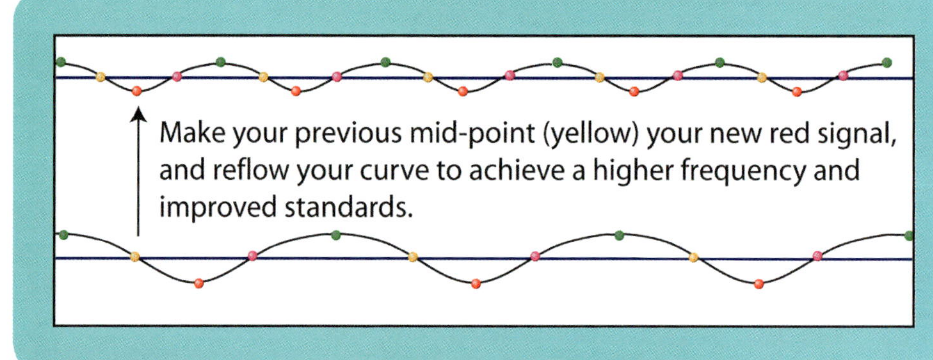

Make your previous mid-point (yellow) your new red signal, and reflow your curve to achieve a higher frequency and improved standards.

4.9 Managing Time

Even though I practice Feng Shui, the art of space arrangement, many clients approach me for advice on how to manage their time. This is probably because people have an intuitive understanding that when they seem to lack time, what they are really lacking is organization in their space.

There are two ways that a lack of organization in the space affects time management:

1. People waste time trying to find things they need. If they need pen and paper, for example, which should be a simple task of reaching for them in the office, becomes a ten minute cycle of hurriedly searching for these supplies, then you cannot be as productive.

2. An unorganized space makes it harder for people to concentrate, and a lack of concentration means reduced efficiency while working, which in turn extends the length of time that tasks take.

If you feel you lack time, take a look at your space and consider how it is affecting your ability to perform needed tasks, and how it may be affecting your ability to think clearly.

Four types of tasks

Not all tasks on our mental list of "to-do's" are equal in importance or need, but many times it is hard for us to decide what are the priorities and how we should organize our time to be most efficient.

Stephen Covey, author of *The Seven Habits of Highly Effective People* popularized the concept of a Time Management Matrix for prioritizing tasks.

He combines the concepts of Urgent and Important in four quadrants:

Important / Urgent	**Important/Not Urgent**
Not Important/Urgent	**Not Important/Not Urgent**

Obviously, things that are both important and urgent have the highest priority. One example of this would be to pay the mortgage, that is due on the first day of the month. Not doing so means that you may face late fee charges. (You may have a grace period, but you would definitely not want to go beyond the date the grace period expires.)

Things that are important, but not urgent come second. Unfortunately, these are easy to leave for later, because we do not feel enough pressure to do them.

If a task is not important, but urgent, you should consider if it is worth doing at all. For example, say that you got a receipt at the store that gives you a chance to enter a giveaway in exchange for doing a survey, and that the code on the receipt expires in three days. This would be urgent, but are the odds of you ever winning this sweep stake enough to justify the investment of the fifteen minutes of your time that taking the survey would take? You decide.

Things that are not important and not urgent should only be considered if they would provide you or someone you love great joy. When I work with clients I find that their to-do items that are not important and not urgent fall into two categories:

1. Items that are perceived as important, but really aren't.

2. Items that are important to someone else, but not the person himself or herself.

For the first set of items I recommend that clients revise their values and their priorities to figure out what really matters to them. For the second, I urge clients to assess the importance of the relationship with the person that is wanting them to do the tasks, and to weigh in the resistance to doing them, with what they lose from the strain in the relationship.

For example, I worked with a client whose wife wanted him to change the carpet. He did not agree that the carpet needed replacing, so to him this item was not important and also not urgent. However, this issue was of extreme importance to his wife, who felt embarrassed about the stains on the carpet when she had company. Because of this embarrassment and because she was very sociable and liked to have people over, she was being passive aggressive towards her husband. He finally understood that even though replacing the carpet was of no importance to him, it was important in keeping the peace in his marriage, and peace was something he valued highly. When he understood this, he became very motivated to replace the carpet.

4.10 The Procrastination List

This is one of the most useful tool I use with clients who are masters at procrastination.

The procrastination list is short, and contains only items that are **important** and **not urgent.** Of all the things we need to do and don't seem to get to, it is those things that are important but not urgent that we tend to avoid. If they were urgent, we would move on them; if they were not important, they would not weigh on us.

Clients are advised to simply look at the list two or three times a day, with no strong purpose or intent to tackle any of the items on the list. Like magic, one day they feel like one of the tasks is very easy to perform and they get it done with a lot less effort than they thought it would have taken.

4.10.1 What We Procrastinate

The things we procrastinate on are those that we perceive as being very difficult in one way or another.

Some of these we may think are difficult because they require great concentration, others because they require we find something we have lost, or that we gather a great amount of information.

Attempting to conquer procrastination with a strong will seems to help very little. I think this is because when we are not or do not feel ready to embark on a project, there is no amount of will that can compensate for that.

4.10.2 Enter the Deeper Mind

Ernest Holmes, one of the proponents of New Thought believed that most of the work of our mind is not done at the conscious level, but at a much deeper level. He calls this profound level of thinking the deeper mind.

The term **deeper mind** is a lot more accurate than the commonly used "unconscious mind" because this part of the mind is always aware. We know that even when a person has lost consciousness, or is "unconscious," the deeper mind is always at work, recording every single thing that happens around the person. We know this because this information can be recovered by hypnosis, or by conscious **returns** to the moment of "unconsciousness."

Someone I know once made a comparison that I find very useful. He said that you could compare the conscious mind to the steering wheel in a semi truck, and the rest of the mechanical parts of the truck are the deeper mind. The job of the steering wheel is to set the direction, but it is the power of the engine , the axles, the tires, etc. that moves the truck and all its contents.

Maxwell Maltz, writer of "Psychocybernetics," taught that once we give a target to the deeper mind (he called it the "unconscious mind") the deeper mind works in the background to figure out how to take us there.

Our job is simply to set the targets, and then allow the deeper mind to do the heavy lifting of thinking. This work is done in the background, and the deeper mind gives signals to the conscious mind when we are ready for the task.

I believe it is because of this mechanism for work of the deeper mind that the procrastination list works so well.

I believe it is because of this mechanism for work of the deeper mind that the procrastination list works so well.

4.10.3 Make a Procrastination List

These are the rules for making and using a procrastination list:

- Keep your list between 4 and 9 items. We have found that 7 items is ideal.
- Look at your list first thing in the morning and right before you go to sleep. If you wish, add one viewing after lunch.
- Do not try to use your will to complete any of these tasks. Remember, you only write in items that are not urgent on this list.
- Take action only when a task feels like it would be really easy to perform. Some people report feeling slightly elated when they read the item on the day they are ready to tackle it. Other people feel that the item slightly shines or seems more visible than the others.
- When you check out one item replace it as soon as you can. The purpose is not to end with an empty list. This is a process that helps us continually tackle actions **that we find difficult to confront.**

A procrastination list is a "to-Do" list that ONLY holds things you have been avoiding doing.

You look at the list morning and night with no intention to perform these tasks. This serves as a reminder for your deeper mind that these tasks need to get done, so that the deeper mind can work on them and the logistics around them **in the background.**

Your deeper mind will let you know when you are ready to do a task. You will feel like it suddenly has become easy to do something that seemed overwhelming before, or you will feel happy and enthusiastic about tackling the chore.

To Do's:

- ☐ *Do taxes.*
- ☐ *Hem pants.*
- ☐ *Research water filters for kitchen.*
- ☐ *Take donations to thrift store.*
- ☐ *Declutter attic.*
- ☐ *Have watch repaired.*
- ☐ *Clean oven.*

Declutter Your Own Spaces

Step

Work with [and not against] the Elements

The five elements are essences or movements that explain the relationships between all things in the world. They connect the life areas with emotions and with the body.

Understanding the elements and how they work can be helpful as we declutter and organize.

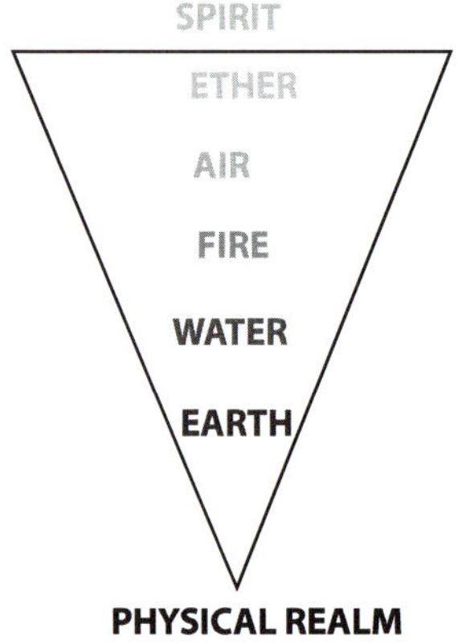

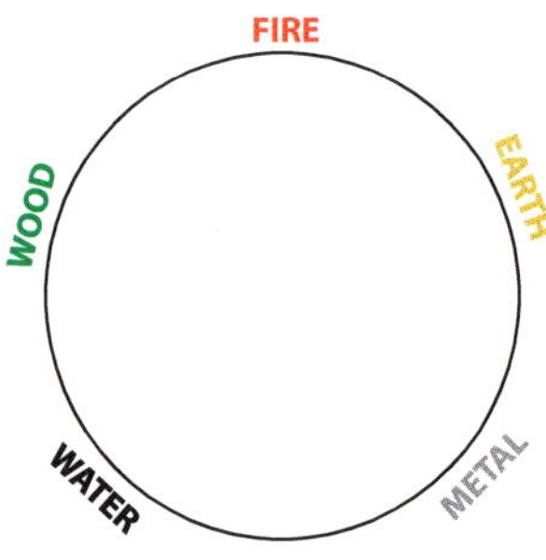

The five elements as they are known in the West have a vertical relationship with each other.

The five elements in the East have a circular relationship with each other.

These two systems are different. Even when the words match in both systems the meanings are not the same. For example, earth in the Western system represents the aspect of reality that has become solid to the touch, but in the Eastern system, the term earth relates to the soil in agriculture.

STEP FIVE: Use the Elements

The Five Elements or Five Phases are movements of energy that regulate the interactions between all that exists. Unlike the elements known in Western culture (ether, air, fire, water and earth) which represent a vertical, hierarchical relationship, the Five Eastern Elements (water, wood, fire, earth and metal) have a horizontal and circular relationship, in a system of checks and balances.

Before we review the way the elements interrelate with each other, let's review what they are:

The water element is symbolized by the wave. It represents flowing energy. Water adopts the shape of the container that holds it and always looks for the easiest course in nature. The season when this element is strongest and predominant is the Winter. The abstract shape that represents it is the oval, and the colors that evoke it are deep blue and black (the deeper you dive, the darker it gets).

The wood (or tree) element is symbolized by the tree and it represents vegetable life on the planet. The season when this element is strongest and predominant is the Spring. The abstract shape that represents it is a tall rectangle, and the colors that evoke it are all the shades of green.

The fire element is symbolized by the flame. It represents the energy of heat, coming from the molten center of the earth or reaching our planet from the sun. The season when this element is strongest and predominant is the Summer. The abstract shape that represents it is the triangle, and the colors that evoke it are red and orange.

The earth element is symbolized by soil and it represents the nutrients that earth delivers to the vegetable kingdom, furthering agriculture and the building of dwellings. The abstract shapes that represent it are the square and the horizontal rectangle, as these are the shapes in which land is divided in plots for cultivating or lots for building, and the colors that evoke it are brown, beige, yellow and tan.

The metal element represents the hardest parts of nature, but which are at the same time malleable and can be melted into all kinds of different shapes. Due to their hardness and because they can be carved into various shapes, rocks are considered part of the metal element. Natural crystals and gems are also part of this element. The season when metal is strongest and predominant is the Fall. The abstract shape that represents it is the circle, and the colors that evoke it are white, gray and mauve (pale purple).

5.1 The Three Cycles of the Five Elements

When placed in a certain order, the elements can support and nurture each other, producing evolution and growth. In the graphic below this order is expressed in the red arrows. When you reverse this order, expressed in the blue arrows, that cycle is reversed so that the elements control each other and the whole cycle slows down and decreases. The

The red arrows indicate the Nurturing Cycle of the Five Elements

The blue arrows indicate the Controlling Cycle of the Five Elements

The black arrows indicate the Destructive Cycle of the Five Elements

WATER feeds WOOD

WOOD feeds FIRE

FIRE produces EARTH

EARTH yields METAL

METAL carries WATER

Every single element is considered the "mother" of the element that follows it clockwise (on the elements wheel), and this applies to the colors of the elements too:

WATER IS THE MOTHER OF WOOD

WOOD IS THE MOTHER OF FIRE

FIRE IS THE MOTHER OF EARTH

EARTH IS THE MOTHER OF METAL

METAL IS THE MOTHER OF WATER

five pointed star in the middle of the graphic, with the black arrows, shows the destructive cycle of the elements. This cycle represents the relationships in which the elements stop each other, and is some times necessary, when there is an excess of one element.

5.2 The Five Elements and Emotions

Each of the five elements is connected with a balanced emotion and two unbalanced emotions. These unbalanced emotions represent the hyper (too much) and the hypo (too little) expressions of the element.

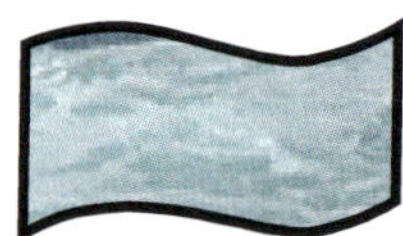

The water element, when it is balanced, produces responsibility, which in Feng Shui is considered an emotional state. When the water element is weak there is fear. When the water element is over the top, there is recklessness.

The wood (or tree) element is expressed in decision, which is also considered an emotional state. When the element is weak, there is indecision, when it is hyper, you find anger.

The fire element, when healthy, is expressed in the joy of living. When low, there is despondency, apathy. When too high, there is workaholism.

The earth element is expressed as reflection when it is balanced. When it is hypo, there is worry. When it is hyper, there is obsession.

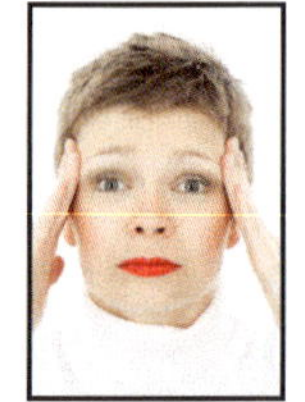

The metal element, when healthy, expresses as nostalgia – that bitter sweet feeling when connecting with the past. Grief is the expression of a weak metal element. Cynicism happens when the metal element is out of bounds.

5.2.1 Decluttering and the Water Element

In Feng Shui, the water element rules life area number one: **Career, Life Mission and Individuality,** located in the middle of the wall that holds the main entrance.

NOTE: see step 8 for the location of all the life areas in the bagua map and in the floor plan.

Any items that are delivered to your home in a periodic or rhythmic manner are related to the water element. This includes magazines, newspapers, newsletters, bulletins, and any subscriptions that you have delivered to your email address. In today's age, formidable amounts of information are received by the average person, and much of this information may be perceived by the individual as being extremely important and worth keeping in case it might be of use some time in the future.

I once worked with a doctor that was at the moment working as a teacher in a University, having given up his private practice. He had not been financially successful running his own practice, and had opted for the security of a salaried job, but he was not sure that there would not be a time in the future when he would want to give private business another try. For this reason he kept several boxes of magazines and newspapers that contained articles about business and managing a medical practice that he thought might be useful in the future. He was **afraid** that if he recycled these materials **he might never come across them again**.

I helped him recognized that the availability of materials on the internet is becoming greater every day, and that there is very little information one could not find if using the right search words. We first tried a strategy by which he would tear out the articles worth keeping and then save them in a three-ring binder.

This task turned out to be daunting, so next I encouraged him to look through his publications and make a note of the authors' names only, so that if one day he felt he needed this information again, he could look it up easily. This turned out to a much better approach for him. He did this for a while, but then realized that his main motivation was fear, and that keeping the information was not worth the work and it was definitely not worth the clutter!

Try this affirmation:

All the information I need finds me at the right moment.

Organizing Clothes:

Clothes should fit right... right now

5.2.2 Decluttering and the Wood Element

The wood element rules two life areas in Feng Shui:

- **Health, Family and Community, and**
- **Wealth, Prosperity and Self-Worth**

The emotion that reflects problems with the wood element is **anger**. The storage space that reflects problems with the wood element is the clothes closet. In Traditional Chinese Medicine, of which Feng Shui forms part, one of the consequences of being unable to handle anger is believed to be weight gain.

An acupunturist shared with me that she rarely met an overweight patient who did not have anger issues. Some of them seemed very jolly and good humored, but it didn't take much searching to find the underlying anger.

I had a client who had been gaining weight with every decade, but never lost the hope that she would "go back" to a previous weight.

As her children each turned 18 and left home, their closets became available to her, and she started moving the clothes that no longer fit her into their closets. Thus she had one closet full of the clothes that fit her in her 40's, and another one with clothes that fit her in her fifties. Now in her early 60's, she was running out of closet space. Because she had so much closet space available to her, she never had to make a decision to let go of her old clothes.

Anger is a very tricky emotion, because if you let it out, you end up hurting others, but if you repress it, you hurt yourself.

As we looked at her clothes, she said she felt angry with herself for allowing her body to get "that big."

Anger is a very tricky emotion, because if you let it out, you end up hurting others, but if you repress it, you hurt yourself.

The upside of anger is decision. The challenge was to help the client turn her anger into decision. I set up a **decluttering prescription** for her, where I instructed her to take out four garments from the closet that held the oldest clothes, every four days. The number four is the number for the life area connected to closets (wealth).

After four weeks, she told me that she was feeling better. A lot of emotions arose as she was working on clearing her closets. It was like taking a trip down memory lane. However, as she finished her fourth week, she felt a new lightness about her, and then she found it easier to let go of more clothes than the original prescription. For example, she noticed that she had a lot of fancy gowns that she used in her forties when she did a lot of volunteering with the local opera. Today, she did not feel any desire to wear this type of clothing. She realized that even if she at some point became able to wear this size clothes again, she would not wear them, so it was easier to let them go. Since they were fine, brand name clothes, she took them to a consignment shop.

Next, she became able to recognize clothes she had kept that looked very old, were worn down or had tears. She was surprised and could not believe that she had kept them. These went into the trash.

She continued the process, becoming more and more aware of how she related to her own body and her self image. She went through a period of feeling angry at herself for putting herself down on account of her weight. When she was 40 she wished she had been happier with the figure she had at 30. When she was 50, she wished she had the figure of her 40 year old self. She imagined herself in her 70's wishing she could go back to her figure at the time of our consultation, then decided to stop being unhappy about the looks of her body, and instead focus on becoming healthier and feeling good inside her skin, just because it was where she lived and not because it was pretty or not. She joined a gym, for the first time seeking health instead of looks.

Interestingly, other types of clutter associated with the wood element are food items, such as are kept in pantries and cabinets and in the refrigerator. Clients find that one way to deal with anger, bitterness or resentments about health and family issues is to clear their food storage spaces from any items that are harmful to them in any way, and especially letting go of expired foods.

5.2.3 Decluttering and the Fire Element

The fire element rules one life area: **Fame, Reputation and Social Life.**

All media, music CDs, movies and video games represent the fire element in the home, because they are often connected with socializing. It is important to only keep those items that you still enjoy, and that you organize them in a way that you can easily find what you are looking for. Music and movies have the power to transport you to other times, but if you feel that when you watched a movie from your past, uncomfortable feelings arise, this may be a sign that you need to let them go or seek healing.

Make sure to let go of obsolete media. For example, if you no longer have a working cassette tape player, what is the point of keeping a collection of cassette tapes? There is almost no past commercial music that cannot be found online. There are also devices that can read from a cassette tape and transfer the music to a CD player or to a computer file, and businesses that offer this service.

By the same token, is there any reason to keep VHS movies if you no longer have a VHS player? If there are any important movies you need to keep, like family movies, get a device that can allow you to transfer to a format that is still in use, such as DVD or Blue Ray, or as a computer file. Maybe there is a friend that can help you with this or a business that can perform this service for you.

Media clutter can **block** fame, reputation and social life.

5.2.4 Decluttering and the Earth Element

Gifts, knick-knacs and books form the clutter that is associated with the earth element.

The earth element rules **Marriage, Relationships, and Partnerships** especially love relationships, learning (reflection), and inner peace.

Do you have in your home objects you do not like but keep them because you are afraid not doing so would hurt the feelings of the person that gave them to you?

Do you keep a closet or cabinet devoted to hiding gifts that you only get out when a friend or relative has announced a visit?

If friends or family members have given you gifts you dislike, there are two questions to ask:

1. Have you not made your thoughts, wishes and likes known to the people around you?

and

2. Are there people in your life that do not respect or care for you enough to find gifts that you would use and like?

These are signs that you are not nurturing **authentic relationships.**

If a family member gives you a gift you do not like but you pretend to like it, you are setting yourself for a lifetime of a dishonest relationship with this person, and a lifetime of getting gifts you do not like from them.

You don't have to be rude or hurt their feelings on purpose, but you may say something like:

"I used to collect teddy bears, and I appreciate your gift, but I am not into them any more. My neighbor has a daughter that is crazy about teddy bears, would you mind if I give it to her?"

Or,

"Thank you so much for your gift, but this color makes me look pale. Would you mind if I exchange it at the store?"

You could also accept a gift graciously, then give it away or donate it. If the person who gave you the gift ever asks you about them, then you can give them a kind, truthful answer.

For example:

"Where s that lamp I gave you for Christmas?" they might ask.

Your possible answer: "It was a very beautiful lamp, but we didn't have where to put it. Our furniture style is contemporary, and the lamp was vintage. I hope you don't mind, I donated it to the church auction. The person who got it felt very blessed."

If your friend or relative gets upset, you may add, "I am sorry this upsets you and I know that you bought the lamp with love, but would you rather I not tell you the truth?"

Sometimes, people may need a little time to come to grips with these honest replies, but relationships worth keeping would not let go of the friendship because you did not like a gift.

Books represent how you relate to life – your beliefs, your hopes, your fears.

Do you keep books that no longer represent who you are or who you want to be?

Relationships worth keeping would not let go of the friendship because you did not like a gift.

Do you keep books that make you feel like the world is a hopeless place?

The world is the way it is, but the way you relate to the world is your choice.

Keep only the books that reflect who you are and who you wish to be, and that help you have a good outlook about the world and your place in the whole of life.

5.2.5 Decluttering and the Metal Element

The metal element rules two life areas:

- **Children, Creativity and Fun, and**
- **Helpful People, Spiritual Life and Travel**

The types of clutter associated with the metal element are the ones related to legal matters, relations with the government, public services, travel, schools and teachers, in short: all paperwork. In the chapter addressing step 9 of this system, you will find strategies to control paperwork.

Cardboard boxes are also part of this type of clutter because they are often associated with getting things in the mail or packing things for moving.

I have helped clients who had an addiction to cardboard boxes and/or shopping bags, thinking that any day they might need them.

A basement full of boxes revealed lots of smaller boxes kept inside, no actual items that were stored in them. This client grew up very poor and now had become very successful – pretty boxes were such treasures when she was a child, and sometimes the only toys for her and her siblings.

A basement full of shopping bags held in each one of them the only happy memories of a childhood – vacations were the only time the parents paid attention to my client.

Until the feelings behind the "hoarding" can be addressed, it becomes very difficult to declutter. In cases like this I recommend that clients seek healing before embarking in large decluttering projects.

One alternative, for example, would be to take digital photos of each bag to keep as electronic mementos, that would not clutter the physical space.

The **Decluttering Prescriptions** provided in step 8 can also be very helpful.

When people are unable to deal with clutter related to the metal element, it is often because of feelings of **grief** or **regrets** about the past. Other times, it is lack of confidence in the future.

The purpose of the Feng Shui consultant helping a client with grief issues, is to get the client to start feeling **nostalgia** when thinking about the past. Nostalgia is that bitter-sweet feeling that shows acceptance for the past, for what has been.

Until the feelings behind the "hoarding" can be addressed, it becomes very difficult to declutter.

The elements in the human body

The five elements that are used to harmonize colors in Feng Shui also have an expression in the human body, each of them corresponds to two organs, a system and an extension:

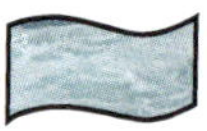

The water element is related to the kidneys and bladder, the bones, the ear and extends to the hair on the scalp.

The wood element is related to the bladder and gallbladder, the muscles, the eyes, and extends the nails.

The fire element is related to the heart and small intestine, and the veins and arteries, and complexion color (cheeks).

The earth element is related to the stomach and spleen, body fat, connective tissues, and extends to the lips.

The metal element is related to the lungs and large intestine, and extends to the skin and bodily hair.

The Five Elements Are Your Helpers!

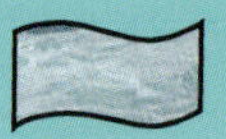

Wash and clean with water - [water element]

Vacuum with wind - [wood element]

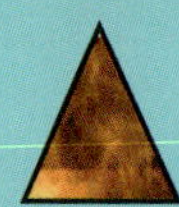

Motivate yourself with fire - [fire element]

Nurture your earth - [earth element]

Polish your metals - [metal element]

Declutter Your Own Spaces

Step

Understand What Different Types of Clutter are Saying

People connect to and understand life through symbols and archetypes.

All the objects in your home or office are giving you some kind of feedback. They are also revealing important things about your life: what you believe, the things that move you, and the fears that stop you.

STEP SIX: Understanding what Clutter Says

Words, symbols and signs are what form **languages**. Languages are used to communicate.

The spaces we inhabit "talk" to us. The careful observation of a room reveals many things about the person who lives or works in it. The "messages" a space sends us are many times literal. For example "a cluttered house reveals a cluttered mind."

Other people and the universe in general "read" the messages that we, our homes and offices send to the world. There is a Chinese saying, "Everything in your home is talking to you, make sure they have nice things to say."

In this section we will explore what the different types of clutter may be saying about your life and what you can do to change messages you do not like.

6.1 Types of Clutter

6.1.1 Stashed-Away Clutter

Clutter disturbs you, so you stash the stuff away. Apparently, your place can look clean and tidy, but... You have a hard time opening drawers because they are so full, closets in general are overflowing, and there's a certain closet or cabinet in the house that you are even afraid to open, either because you don't know what you would find in there or because of the danger of things falling on your head... Or you detour all the clutter into a storage room or a garage (which is so full your car hasn't been inside it for who knows how long).

This kind of clutter might be associated with an inability to confront and evaluate the past (and therefore difficulty learning from past experiences), lack of knowledge of your present resources, assets and possibilities, and uncertainty about the future (afraid of what lies ahead. Reluctant to "open doors" for fear of what might fall on top of you). There may also be a tendency of showing one face to the world while hiding your true self – fear of being unloved if your true self gets through.

Some places give the impression of being tidy because the mess is stashed away behind doors or inside drawers and chests.

6.1.2 Organized Clutter

Maybe you have the ability to find a place for every object that finds its way into your house or office. Everything is organized but crowded. Most of the walls are lined up with storage shelves and cabinets and the remaining surfaces are filled with paintings and/or posters. Shoe boxes or plastic containers are stacked up on top of one another. Bookshelves have double-rows of books. Dusting is a never ending job and there are many places where you can't vacuum easily because the vacuum doesn't fit between pieces of furniture. If your space is like this, you probably feel general tightness and tension in life. You may feel that money is tight, or that your relationships with those close to you are tense because you think you need more freedom, more space. You may perceive life as being full of obstacles and confusing.

It is possible to be very organized while keeping a lot of clutter. For example, you could have a book shelf full of books that do not represent your own outlook on life (mental clutter).

If you don't get rid of things you don't have a need for and don't love, it might also be hard to let go of the past, and the latter is often associated with resentment and being reluctant to forgive. This, of course, excludes valuable collections.

6.1.3 Messiness or Temporary Clutter

Your space may be in general organized and uncluttered, but sometimes you get behind with paperwork, or laundry, or you have been using tools for a definite purpose, and don't immediately put them back in their place; or your children leave toys laying around. All of these account for a messy aspect. Every so often you go through the house picking up, putting away, throwing away, and once again your place looks neat and tidy.

A messy place can make you feel tired, overwhelmed and stressed out. You are probably afraid that things could go out of control at any minute.

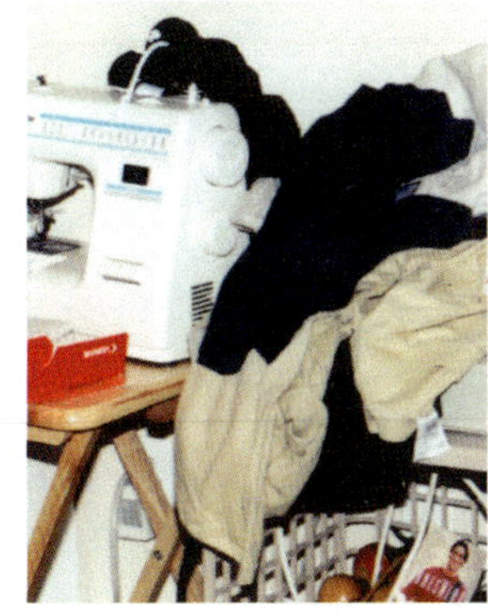

In Feng Shui we are not concerned with messes, that could be cleared with a little concentration and work, as much as with stagnation, created by clutter that remains unpicked for a long time.

6.1.4 Chaos

Chaos is a combination of accumulation and disorder. If you are living in a chaotic space, you are probably often confronted with confusion and anxiety or even desperation. Because you have lost track of what you have, it becomes very hard to let anything leave the house, for fear of being left without, or losing something important. Likewise, you may be holding on to old grudges for fear of being left unprotected if you drop your guard. On the other hand, you may be buying things you already have because you have forgotten about them or because you can't find them. Your ability to make objective decisions may be affected. Frustration and rage are not uncommon, but apathy can also be present—the desire to give up because "What's the point"?

6.1.5 Hidden Order

Some people live perfectly comfortably in a messy place, which though it appears to be in disorder, has a certain organization apparent only to its inhabitant. He or she knows where everything is and manages to be effective. They often seem to do very little but in the end they accomplish a great deal. If you are one of these people, you probably feel that others do not give you the recognition or trust you deserve. You probably have the reputation of being "light headed." You invest so much time and energy keeping track of your stuff you sometimes forget simple things or make foolish mistakes.

6.1.6 Well-Intentioned Clutter

Over-accesorizing can also create clutter. A common example is to place too many pillows on a bed. Many people do this because these arrangements look really good at the store, but they are very inconvenient for ordinary life.

Sometimes, women tend to over-accessorize a room with too many pillows, lace and plush dolls. It may look cute and cozy, but it is uncomfortable if guests cannot sit on the couch unless they remove two or three pillows, or if your husband finds the bed already occupied by Teddy bears.

6.1.7 Excessive Order

Yes, there is such thing as being too clean, or too organized. I've seen people destroy the finish of their cabinets because they scrubbed too hard or they used cleaning agents that were too strong. Compulsive cleaners/organizers despair when somebody moves their stuff around or does not return things to their place... they agonize if the children or the dog bring in dirt from the outside. If you live or work in a place where rules are too rigid, you probably feel lack of freedom, are afraid of being judged, and may have suppressed your creativity. If you are the one setting the rules, you might organize yourself into intolerance and lack of compassion or act with insensitivity towards the needs and desires of those around you.

6.1.8 Lack of Adornments

Some people, who have a hard time with housekeeping chores, opt for a simplified look: nothing but the essential pieces of furniture, so that vacuuming will be a breeze. No adornments to dust, not a single nail on the walls. Such people may experience lack of joy and their creative energy may be overpowered by their practicality. Beware also of "color themes." Too much color coordination throughout the house may indicate preponderance of one or two of the five elements over the others and rooms may lack character.

6.1.9 Unclosed Cabinets and Drawers

Unexpected open drawers and/or cabinet doors can become potential weapons against heads, shoulders and thighs. When the drawers are low, one could even trip on them and fall, causing varying degrees of injury. This habit could indicate a difficulty in closing deals or a tendency to leave things unfinished. Some people with memory problems leave cabinet doors and drawers open because otherwise they tend to forget what's in them. Men will do this in areas with which they are not very familiar i.e. the kitchen (if they don't cook and don't know where everything is). A good solution for this is discreetly but clearly labeling cabinet doors and drawers. Labeling also helps in closet or storage areas, and in children's rooms to make it easier for them to remember where things belong. But –before doing this– secure the agreement of the other person(s) involved.

6.1.10 Uncleanliness

When you live or work in a place that is not clean, even if you have gotten used to it, certain worries will be present in the back of your mind. You'll be concerned about germs, and the sicknesses they could produce, about pests invading your home, about getting dust or grease on your clothes to name a few. You may also be afraid to invite people into your house out of embarrassment. If the uncleanliness extends to your person you may live with the fear of being rejected or unloved. These feelings will often be accompanied by guilt. Being surrounded by uncleanliness for extended periods of time can make a person feel undeserving, suspicious of other people's intentions or prone to get involved in "dirty" deals.

Uncleanliness may be a symptom of low self esteem.

6.2 Hidden Reasons Why People Clutter

Whenever a person displays any kind of limiting behavior, it is usually a POSITIVE response in an effort to compensate for something else which is perceived by part of the mind as potentially more destructive.

Although people are not textbooks and every case is different, most reasons why we clutter can be reduced to trying to compensate for the following four situations:

6.2.1 A Feeling of Emptiness

Whenever a table, shelf, wall or room looks too bare, we feel like something is missing and we unconsciously try to fill it up. Feelings of emptiness are often related to not following one's path in life, by having a career that does not "fulfill" us. Some people clutter so they can avoid these feelings. It might help to place one or two beautiful objects that attract the attention, but leaving some "breathing" room.

6.2.2 Not Wanting To Confront The Past

It is necessary for us to every once in a while evaluate our pasts in order to project our future, but this means we have to confront both good and bad past experiences, and remembering the latter usually involves emotional pain. Therefore, we let newer things accumulate and cover up the old, to avoid suffering.

6.2.3 Afraid to Face The Future

Having a messy house always gives us "something to do" (clean up and organize), even if we don't ever do it, giving us a wonderful excuse for never really starting the projects we have planned.

6.2.4 Loneliness

Humans were not designed to be reclusive and lonely. We are social beings. We thrive when being nurtured by loving relationships. If these are lacking... it hurts! Clutter can make us numb so that we fool ourselves into thinking that we do not need others.

Clutter is usually a compensation for something else.

Decluttering requires us to face our emotions.

6.3 There Is No Way Around Cleaning and Organizing

During consultations, customers who share their homes or workplaces with messy people frequently ask if there is some kind of "cure" they can use to "override" the other person's clutter or uncleanliness. Unfortunately, there is no such cure.

There is **stagnation** present in spaces that are cluttered or unclean. When we say something is stagnant, this means it is not moving or flowing, and it then becomes stale, dirty, and foul as a consequence. I am sure all of you have experienced at some point in your lives a sense of relief and a sudden, uplifting, invigorating feeling after performing a simple cleaning or organizing task, such as washing the windows in your house or cleaning up a drawer or closet.

Live only with those objects that you use and love.

Manage the clutter in your spaces. Your choices and habits define your environment and your surroundings influence your views on yourself and life as well.

- live only with those objects that you use and love, and that give you a positive feeling about yourself, your loved ones and your life

- emphasize comfort and safety when arranging your rooms, get set up with the right kind of furniture, accessories and lighting for the activities you want to perform in that space.

- visit and straighten out storage areas of your home, office or garden at least once every six months (ideally every three months). This includes storage rooms, sheds, closets, high cabinets, attics, finished and unfinished basements.

But what can you do if people around you refuse to tidy up? First of all, **stop the nagging.** Of course you have a right to be upset and complain, but the question is, does it work? Is the person more willing to change his or her habits because of your irritated comments? Most clutterers will respond to nagging with stubbornness.

Second, try to understand where this person is coming from. People do not overeat so that they can get overweight, or drink alcohol in the hopes of becoming alcoholics, or clutter in order to make themselves or you uncomfortable.

Some people will say that they feel comfortable in a messy place, but usually it is just that they have become numb and do not notice any more how disturbing that can be.

In Feng Shui what's inside - hidden - is more important than what is visible.

Validate and praise any effort of your clutterer friends or relatives to tidy up, even if you do not agree with their particular way of going about it. Offer, but do not impose your help in the process.

If you have the tendency to clutter or to let your place or work area get messy, the following sections may give you some tips on how to identify bad housekeeping habits and replace them with more constructive ones.

However, start by being kind to yourself and do not berate yourself for any real or perceived limitation in keeping your place free of clutter.

Motivate yourself to get a handle on the space around you by focusing on the many benefits of a life with reduced clutter. Many people report that when they reduce clutter:

- It becomes easier to find things.
- It is easier to concentrate.
- It frees up time!

6.4 Tips for Decluttering the House

Start in your bedroom or the room you use most often. Then move on to other rooms.

Watch out for the following:

- Things that are obviously and indisputably rubbish (e.g. clothes tags, outdated newspapers, invitations for events that have already taken place, expired coupons, packaging, etc.). Recycle them or throw them away.
- Things that are broken or damaged beyond repair. Throw them away, recycle them or give them to somebody who can use them for spare parts.
- Things that are broken or malfunctioning but can be repaired — fix them or give them to someone who will.
- Things that work fine, but you don't really use—pass them on to someone who needs them, or take them to your church, the Salvation Army, Good Will, thrift store, etc.
- Things you use but don't like because they are too old, uncomfortable, unsafe, or ugly.

- Things you use and like but were given to you by someone who treated you poorly or didn't mean well—make plans to replace them soon.
- Let go of any other items that evoke negative feelings in you like guilt or resentments, or that bring you bad memories.
- Let go of the things you do not love.
- Let go of the items that no longer represent who you are or who you want to be.

If the task seems too big, start with one object, deal with it, and then choose another object and deal with it. One by one, until you feel more comfortable and secure to handle other chores.

If you have difficulty throwing or giving away things, take an intermediate step: put them in two big cardboard boxes (mark them: "things to recycle or throw away" and "things to give away").

If you find it hard to get the boxes, two heavy duty trash bags will do. These will give you the opportunity of looking through them if you change your mind about a certain object before it leaves your house.

Yard or garage sales are OK as long as they take place fast (within three months of your decision to start decluttering the house), otherwise, you will be better off just giving those objects away.

For especially challenging cases, keep in mind that there are professionals who clean and organize people's places for a living; they are a great option, for example, when job schedules make it hard for us to perform all the necessary house chores, or when it has become our responsibility to organize someone else's place and we find it hard to confront it emotionally.

Expect to feel a sensation of emptiness or regret as you clear clutter. This is natural. In a short time, this process will reduce your tendencies to give in to negative emotions, and you will start feeling better and stronger. Your mind will be clearer and your heart lighter.

Remember: you are making room for chi, the life force to run more freely through the different spaces of your home or business and this will create better conditions for a thriving life.

6.5 The Order of Healing and Cleansing

During true healing processes, the body expels toxins from top to bottom, from the inside to the outside, and from back to front.

Follow similar guidelines when cleaning the house. The more private spaces need to be addressed first because they are more "internal."

In each room, start with the cabinets, drawers or shelves where you keep the most personal items. If decluttering a chest of drawers, start with the top drawer and then work your way down.

Organize rooms in this order: the bedroom you sleep in; the other bedrooms in the house; the bathroom; then the home office (if you have one); the kitchen; living and dining areas; outside storage rooms; garages; and carports.

6.6 Chaotic Active Space

This relates to messiness in an area you use regularly. We are talking extreme chaos here. You find it hard to even get into the room, but yet you have to because this is where you work, or where you sleep.

A chaotic room indicates a state of confusion, and this is how you tackle it:

1. Stand in the middle of the room, look around you on the floor and pick up ONE item that is indisputably trash. Put it in a bag or box labeled "trash." Stand up in the middle of the room again and repeat the procedure. Do this seventeen times.

2. Stand in the middle of the room, look around you, giving special attention to shelves, tables and dressers. Identify ONE object that is broken, torn or damaged beyond the possibility of repair. Put it in a bag or box labeled: "broken beyond fixing." Stand in the middle of the room again and repeat the procedure. Do this thirteen times.

3. Stand in the middle of the room and look around you on the floor. Identify ONE item that you LOVE, pick it up and place it safely on a bed or couch. Stand in the middle of the room again and repeat the procedure. Do this seventeen times.

4. Stand in the middle of the room, look around you, giving special attention to shelves, tables and dressers. Identify ONE object that is OK, but you do not use or do not like and put it in a bag or box labeled

"to give away." Stand in the middle of the room again and repeat the procedure. Do this thirteen times.

5. Stand in the middle of the room, look around you, on the floor and furniture and identify ONE item that no longer represents who you are or who you want to be. Put it in the bag or box labeled "to give away." Stand in the middle of the room again and repeat the procedure. Do this nine times.

Repeat steps from 1-5 three times and you should be done. As you go along it will get easier. You can get someone else to coach you while you do this, but it is better that they DON'T physically help you, since you attention will be distracted wondering what they are doing, and worrying that they may be throwing away something you want to keep.

6.7 Putting One Room in Order

This is a procedure for a room that you have already decluttered, and just gotten messy.

1. Start by scanning the room and pick up all the "throwables," items that belong in the trash can or recycling bin. Route them to the proper container.

2. Scan the room again and locate any items that do not belong in that room. Pick up items one by one and take them to their places. Tip: do not fall into the temptation of tidying up the room where you took a certain object, if you do, you will loose your focus.

3. Then locate any items that belong to the room but are not in their proper places. Put them back in their places.

4. Next straighten out items that even though they are in their proper places, have been moved or look askew.

5. What you will be left to deal with are what I call "undefinable" items. Those objects that have no place, that you are not sure who they belong to, and don't know whether to keep them or throw them out or give them away.

6. When organizing, start from the floor up.

7. When cleaning, start from the top down.

When cleaning, work from the top down.

When picking up, work from the floor up.

6.8 The Junk Room

This applies not only to over-cluttered storage rooms or garages, but also to "stuffed" closets and overfilled drawers, and this is the best solution:

GET EVERYTHING OUT OF THERE

Engage the help of healthy strong friends, or hire help. Take every safety precaution. You will be dealing with stagnant and bottled up chi, plus you will be stirring up emotions as you take that trip down memory lane. Under these circumstances it is easy to get distracted.

If even the slightest injury results (paper cut, wood splinter, etc.), have every member of the party take a break and go outside for a breath of fresh air for a few minutes.

Before you put any item back in the storage room (or closet or drawer) ask yourself:

- **Do I use it?**
- **Do I love it?**
- **Is it truly a heirloom?**

Put an item back only if you answered yes to these three questions and do this only after cleaning it up. Consider wearing gloves and/or masks if you have allergies or are sensitive to dust.

6.9 Handling Attics and Basements

Major decluttering jobs, such as cleaning up attics, basements and storage rooms (this includes garages that are being used as junk rooms) can be hard to confront because they seem overwhelming. If you have help and the weather is good you can follow the advice to deal with junk rooms on this page. If you must tackle the project by yourself follow this procedure:

From the access door start removing items in order to create a passage way from there to the back wall. Then remove objects from the center of this "corridor" to the sides, so that you can open up a cross of circulation in the attic, basement or storage room. Once you have achieved this you know you can go in any moment and retrieve and take out objects one by one at your own pace. Have some big cardboard boxes (or industrial strength trash bags) marked:

- Things to throw away
- Things to donate
- Things to distribute among family members
- Things to fix for use
- Things to fix and then store again
- Items related to family history that I want to keep

Remember that the secret to great storage is "NOTHING ON THE FLOOR" (except for items that were designed to be on the floor).

6.10 Clearing Electro-Magnetic Pollution

Electromagnetic pollution is becoming prevalent.

Years ago only people who lived very close to electric power plants or towers needed to be concerned with exposure to electromagnetic pollution.

Today, with the prominent use of cell phones and the ever increasing use of wireless networks, most people are being exposed to EMFs.

For this reason it is necessary for us to do two things:

1. Counteract the effects of EMFs.
2. Increase our immunity to EMFs.

6.10.1 Counteracting EMFs

Even though cell phone companies and service providers, as well as electric companies insist that there is no evidence that EMFs cause any threat to health, there are many people who claim that they feel tired or drained when exposed to EMFs.

In the world of vibrational or energetic healing, EMFs are believed to disrupt the natural flow of the human energy field, or aura.

One way to counteract the effects of EMFs is to do the things that promote a healthy flow of chi in the human energy field. These are:

Contact with the Earth

- If you live by a beach, take a walk on the sand at least once a week.
- If you live in an area where it is safe to lie down on the grass (no fire ants or other problematic insects), place a cotton blanket or sheet on the grass and lie down on it. Do this at least once per week.

Shielding

There are numerous products out there that claim to protect from EMFs:

- **Products you can wear,** like bracelets, Teslar watches, or pendants.
- **Home protection devices.** These come in the shape of items you can plug to your electric system which claim to neutralize or reduce EMFs.
- **Ceramic based paint** may help filter EMFs in rooms located in homes that are close to electrical plants or electrical towers.

Research items well before making purchases and see if you can contact people who have used them and have had good results.

Choices

Choices we make in our purchases and lifestyle can make a difference in our exposure to EMFs.

- If you have decided to no longer use incandescent light bulbs, **do not** switch to fluorescent bulbs. Fluorescent bulbs have a number of problems: higher electromagnetic emissions, intermittent light (can cause migraines and even trigger epileptic attacks), they contain mercury and may be toxic when broken, and unless you purchase the more expensive "full spectrum" lights, they have a limited range of light that causes the eyes to strain. A much better alternative are **LED** (light emitting diode) lights. They have a wider range of visible light and color that are very pleasant to the human eye, they consume less electricity and last longer than fluorescent lights.

- You can also choose to work on computers and other electronic devices for shorter periods of time, or taking more frequent breaks.

- Choose to not take electronic devices inside the bedroom, or take them in only for limited periods of time. If you keep a computer or tablet in the bedroom, cover up the screen before going to bed. If you need to keep a cell phone on your night stand, try putting it inside a drawer or on the edge of the night stand opposite the bed.

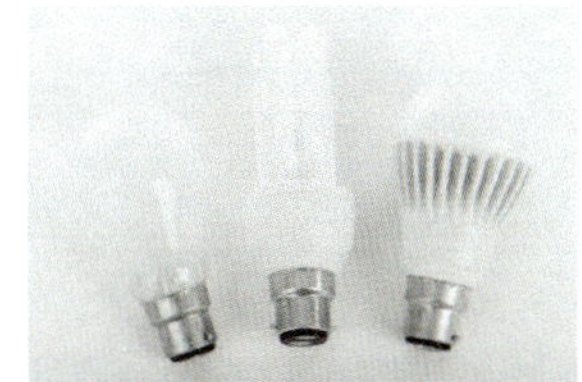

It is a great idea to switch light bulbs in order to reduce the carbon footprint and save money on electricity, but fluorescent lights are bad choices for more than one reason, including that they are "bad Feng Shui."

LED lights are Feng Shui correct, consume less electricity than fluorescent bulbs, and last longer.

Spiritual Immunity

When working with clients I have found that often their fears and worries about EMFs make them even more vulnerable to their influence. I have observed that clients who are very afraid of EMFs get headaches when taking on cell phones, and their ear gets red and hot to the touch, whereas clients who love their cell phones, do not seem to suffer any immediate ill effects.

What is more interesting is that I have observed that when talking on the phone with people who believe "cell phones are killing them" my own ear sometimes got red and hot to the touch, but when I talk with healer friends who have a very high vibration and love technology, I do not have any problems when talking with them on the same cell phone.

It is important to work on increasing our spiritual immunity against EMFs. I believe that by keeping our vibration high we make it less likely to be adversely affected by them.

For this purpose, healer Bill Austin and I have created a spiritual healing and clearing method called **Angelic Feng Shui Training,** which deals with subtle Feng Shui issues, including vulnerabiity to EMFs.

All the light switches and outlets in my home have the Angelic Feng Shui stickers on them.

These help uplift the energy of my home and help me build spiritual immunity to EMFs.

With Angelic Feng Shui:

- You can get the Angelic Feng Shui lotus flower stickers to place on all electrical switches and outlet plates. This image contains the vibrational healing artwork created by Bill Austin with the intent from the healing and clearing vibrations of this modality.
- You can play the Angelic Feng Shui recordings, available on CD or MP3 to clear the spiritual ill effects of EMFs from your home or office every day. These recordings are also very helpful to help deal with fear or anxiety when exposed to information that tends to elicit those emotions, such as the news.
- You can purchase the training so that you get the spiritual attunement for Angelic Feng Shui training. Feedback we have gotten from people who have been attuned for Angelic Feng Shui suggests that they find it easier to coexist with electro-magnetic pollution and are also more aware to shield themselves in other ways, and to counteract the effects by being more in nature.

www.angelicfengshuitraining.com

Declutter Your Own Spaces

Step

Maintaining Physical, Emotional and Energetic Spatial Health

A basic level of physical, emotional and energetic wellbeing is strongly connected with how we take care of the spaces around us. By consciously intending to keep the gears turning in our physical, emotional and spiritual worlds we create environments where it becomes easier to be healthy and happy.

STEP SEVEN: Maintaining Physical, Emotional and Energetic Health

Traditional Chinese Thought, which is the basis for both Traditional Chinese Medicine and Feng Shui considers that everything happens in three levels of existence:

• Heaven

• Earth

• Humankind

Heaven deals with the things that are beyond the physical universe and manifest in our minds as thoughts.

Earth is related to the physical world – this three dimensional reality where things require time to take place and where things happen as a response to energy.

Humankind refers to the energy of life, and it manifests as the emotions that motivate human beings to get ideas from Heaven and work on Earth to produce effects in the physical universe. Humans are considered the connectors of heaven and earth.

To keep a home healthy, all three levels need to be addressed.

7.1 Keep the Gears Turning (Earth Level)

In the physical universe what doesn't improve gets worse, and maintaining is much better than repairing. Create a maintenance schedule for your home to make sure you catch problems before they get expensive. Include maintenance for the furnace, air conditioning, water heater and the roof. You may also want to add maintenance schedules to appliances.

There is a part of our personality that does not reason, but acts based on experience, instinct, and desire. This part of our *Selves* has often been compared to animals or to small children. Its main goal is self preservation. Some experts call it the basic personality or the basic self, or the inner child. The inner child bases its reactions on the information gathered through the five physical senses.

Check your house or office for safety, as if a two year old or a very intoxicated person were walking through it. Whatever poses a potential threat to any of the two, will certainly be read as impending danger by your inner child.

Check your house or office for safety, as if a two year old or a very intoxicated person were walking through it.

7.1.1 All Items In Your House Ought to Be in Good Condition and Working Properly

Items that malfunction or do not work at all are easily identified with danger and death. To say the least, they are a sign of deterioration and carelessness. Keeping them is "Bad Feng Shui."

On the other hand, things that are in good condition and working properly are signs of prosperity and unconsciously relate to security and good health.

Functionality does not only apply to proper operation, but also to whether we use an item or not. **If we never use an object, then it is not working.** If you have items that you have not used for more than **a year and one season,** you probably do not need them and it may be a good idea to let them go. Either sell them or give them to someone who will use them.

Deterioration and despondency are fast slides on steep hills. Stay on top of this situation. Repair or replace any malfunctioning, broken or torn items as quickly as you can. The longer you wait, the harder it will be, due to loss of momentum.

Eventually you may end up getting used to living with broken items. Every torn or nonworking item is a small source of nuisance. The accumulation of these increases the tensions inside the household and the latter may lead to more arguments.

These problems in the home drain the energy you need for life.

Take charge. Keep the gears of your home or office turning and running smoothly. You may find that endeavors in other areas of life yield more results as well, and faster.

7.1.2 Take care of these obvious physical needs for repair, that we sometimes overlook

- Fix leaks.
- Replace broken glass in windows and mirrors.
- Wash or touch-up stains on walls, or paint the whole room or house, if needed.
- Remove stains from carpets and other kinds of floor coverings, or patch them up.
- Glue, nail or tighten bolts and screws on wobbly beds, chairs and tables.
- Make sure all doors and drawers open and close smoothly, fully and noiselessly.
- Have nonworking appliances repaired.

In addition:

- Make sure all clocks and watches in the house and office are working properly.
- Let your calendars reflect the right month.

7.1.3 A healthy building has:

- A sound physical structure (foundation, columns, beams, supporting walls, staircases, roof, etc.)
- Good condition of the systems (electrical, plumbing, heating, air conditioning, gas lines, etc.)

The condition of every item in your home is your responsibility, whether you do things yourself or hire outside help.

- Proper upkeep and function of elements that open and close, such as doors, windows, cabinet doors and drawers, and that of any built-in elements like closets.

- Wall and floor coverings that are clean and properly maintained (paint, wallpaper, carpet, wood, tile, etc.).

The furnishings of a building are also part of the health of a home:

- The furniture, which should be in good condition, comfortable, functional and safe.

- The condition and cleanliness of artwork hanging from the walls, curtains and other kinds of window treatments (like blinds) and that of rugs and mats on the floor.

7.2 CLEARING EMOTIONS (HUMANKIND LEVEL)

Emotions connect our thoughts with our actions at the physical level. Our emotions can also be subtly affected by items that surround us.

Make sure to choose artwork and ornaments that help you have good feelings. Avoid any images or objects that have a tendency to produce negative emotions, such as fear, anger or worry.

- Remove from the home images that reflect war, poverty or any other types of struggle. In some business settings images like these may be OK if they are in alignment with the mission or purpose of the business or organization, but avoid them in the areas where you work, such as your personal office or cubicle.

- Remove any images that have distorted or contorted human figures. These may be OK in some business settings, but are not auspicious in a home. For example, most paintings by the French artist Renoir would be considered desirable in Feng Shui, but most paintings pertaining to the cubist period of the Spanish painter Picasso would not be considered good Feng Shui for a home.

- Make sure there are no mirrors that fragment, distort or deform the image in any way. This includes tile mirrors, convex or concave

Happy, peaceful images elicit good responses.

Unhappy or scary images can stir up negative emotions.

Mirrors that split or distort images give the wrong feedback about life. They are considered inauspicious.

Bevels may be considered chic or elegant, but they are bad Feng Shui.

mirrors and even the bevels on the countour of many mirrors. These are considered inauspicious because they do not provide an accurate reflection of reality.

- Pay special attention to the stories that displayed photographs are telling about the home or business. What would a person that walks into the space for the first time assume about the people living or working in this space? If the story told by photographs is not true to life, this will weaken your relationships with family or co-workers.
- Make sure that all the people in a home or business have some place over which they have control in terms of aesthetics, even if it is just one wall or bulletin board. People need to express themselves and allowing expression in the space is symbolic of allowing expressions in life.
- Never display photos that embarrass a family member or a co-worker.
- Beware of any ornaments or artwork with sharp angles, where people could get hurt. It is better not to have any object that would be potentially hazardous, but if this cannot be helped, place them away from paths, where people would not be at risk of hitting them accidentally.

The state of our spaces does reflect our inner state, but there is no point in getting upset at ourselves because we find clutter.

It is a better idea to focus on the improvements we can generate in our space that will help us feel better about ourselves and our lives.

7.2.1 Quick Feng Shui Cures for Negative States of Heart

Feeling Stuck - in a job, relationship, in a particular problem, at school, etc. First, make sure that all clocks and watches in the house are working properly and showing the right time. Second, check all drawers and cabinet doors and make sure they open and close properly (that they don't get stuck). Tighten up screws, add oil and sand and buff where necessary.

Feeling Blue - First, open all doors and windows, if the weather allows it, to let the air flow. Second, pick up nine items that are on the floor and don't belong there, and put them in their place or recycle them/throw them away (whichever applies).

Feeling Anxiety - First, get out of the house and walk for twenty minutes. Second, look for four objects in your home that you totally dislike and give them away.

Feeling Fear - First, close all curtains and blinds. Second, put away all potentially dangerous objects, like scissors, knives, blades, etc., then open blinds and curtains again.

Feeling Rejected - First, take out of your closet and give or throw away four items of clothing that don't really flatter you. Second, groom yourself, shave, pluck, brush, clip, bathe, apply lotions, oils, perfumes... spend three hours in front of the mirror, like when you were a teen.

Feeling Lonely - First, put on some music that you find very comforting. Second, organize those photos that haven't made their way into photo albums or boxes yet.

Feeling Discouraged - First, light up some candles or incense. Second, look around the house for five items that represent past achievements and place them in more visible places.

Not Knowing What to Do Next - Pick up your shoes and put them away. Shoes thrown about, all pointing in different directions, resemble confusion about life's directions.

Feeling Like a Failure - Take a look at your photo albums.

Feeling Low Self -Esteem - Place *more* mirrors around the place. Choose mirrors with no bevels and no distortions — good quality mirrors in nice frames.

Feeling Angry - Put that destructive energy to good use: pull weeds from your lawn or garden; or take out the trash and set the intent to throw out your anger with it.

Feeling Guilty - Do your laundry.

Feeling Tired - Change the sheets. Optional: flip/rotate the mattress.

Feeling Resentful - Let old things go, those things that look too old or which you do not use any more.

Angelic Feng Shui Training

Angelic Feng Shui is a Healing and Clearing Modality created by Moni Castaneda and Vibrational Healer Bill Austin.

Angelic Feng Shui makes **vibrational energetic corrections** for Feng Shui issues that are hard to resolve by physical means, while also addressing and clearing subtle energetic problems in home, work and outdoors environments.

Angelic Feng Shui is especially useful:

- When dealing with the effects of EMFs (electromagnetic frequencies) and/ or Geopathic Stress (natural discordant energies).
- When dealing with less-than-love energies, frequencies or entities.
- When a physical Feng Shui Cure is very difficult or impossible to apply.

angelicfengshuitraining.com

7.3 CLEARING SUBTLE ENERGIES (HEAVEN LEVEL)

Start by checking the energy level, including:

- The state of the health and mood of the people who live or work there
- The state of personal belongings of the occupants of the home
- The general smell of the place.
- The condition of live plants and pets – Are they thriving or do they look sickly?
- is the place cluttered or dirty?

Additionally, inquire about the history of the building itself and that of its previous occupants. Watch out for the following:

A. History of ruptured pipes, short-circuits, invasion of plagues of insects or rodents.

B. History of divorce, bankruptcy or violent death in the premises.

If you have proof that undesirable or shocking events occurred at a place, or even if without any evidence you have a strong "feeling" that this is the case, you may need to cleanse the energy of such place.

In Feng Shui, to clear a building from stagnated or sick chi, we use:

- Fire, as in candles, or safely burning alcohol [spirits] in a container,
- Penetrating scents such as incense, essential oils, and lemon or pine scented cleaners, and
- Vibrating sounds like those produced by bells, gongs, reverberating music, clapping...

The clearing cannot be performed in its entirety if the building is not physically cleaned first, as dust, spills and fouls smelling items will keep sick chi in place. In extreme cases, it is better to let go of any furniture with porous materials that may have absorbed the stagnant energy. If the items must be kept, they should be taken outside and exposed to fresh air and sun while they are being cleaned.

If you can, take all the furniture out of a room you are going to clear after an illness or death has occurred there, so that first you can do a "deep" cleansing, with one window and one door open. Once the physical task has been completed, let incense burn (sage is an excellent choice) while you follow the procedure explained in the next few pages.

If you wish, you may enlist the help of a priest, a shaman, or a friend or relative with "excellent luck" to perform the cleansing or clearing of negative chi. Dogs, especially male dogs, can be great companions for clearings.

Odor absorbing agents will also absorb stagnated chi. These can be: a brown paper bag full of charcoal; odor absorbing stones (usually used for basements and which can be reactivated by exposure to the sun); or air purifiers with carbon filters.

We clap three times to state the intention that we are clearing on three levels of existence: Heaven, earth and humankind, or in other words, thoughts, physical action, and the emotions that connect them both.

7.3.1 Using the Seven ANGELIC Healing Rays to Cleanse a Space

There is something mysterious and powerful in walking through a space while clearing stagnant or sick chi by following the path of the seven rays, which makes the process faster and much more effective than just walking in a random way or in a circular motion. See the graphic on page 94.

It is simpler than it looks. In your mind, place the magic numbers in the corners and midpoints of the room and then just follow the numbers (only you begin with "three" instead of "one"): 3 - 4 - 5 - 6 - 7 - 8 - 9 - 1 - 2.

7.3.2 The Cleanse

Before you begin, stand outside of the building or room, clap three times to call the attention of Heaven, Earth and Humankind and announce your intention of going inside to perform a cleanse. Enter the space and light some incense (sage works great) on a heat resistant surface close to the middle of the room or building. For the cleanse you can carry either a candle , or a big feather (a feather duster will work too) **in your right hand.**

Incense, candles, feathers, sage, bells, alcohol, salt... some of the tools you can use to clear stagnant chi.

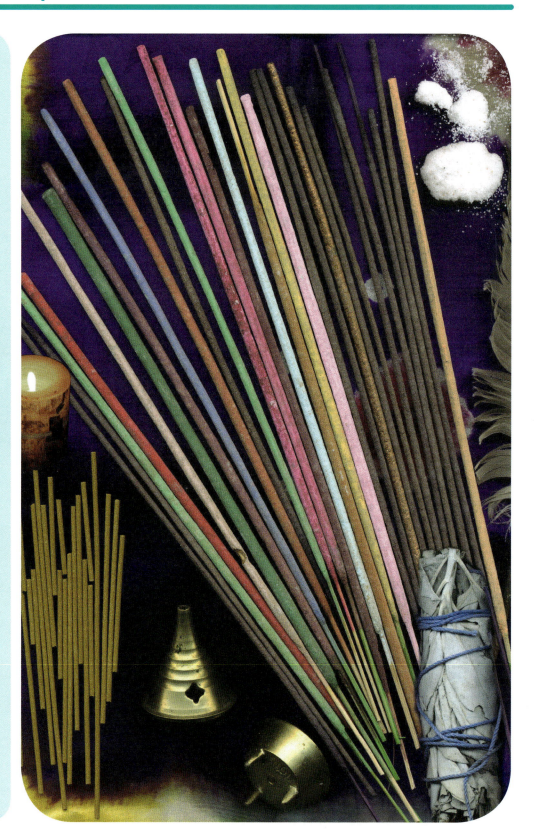

Starting at the point marked with number "three" think about and visualize the circumstances relating to Family, Health and Community that you would like to change. Accept and give thanks for **what is** and what you have learned from it, then release all negativity related to that Life Aspiration, cleaning it symbolically with the feather or "consuming" it in the fire. Ask that all that is cleared is replaced by blessings. Now walk to the corner marked with the number "four."

At number "four" follow the same steps as you did at number "three:" visualize, accept, give thanks and release, only this time focus your attention on "Wealth, Prosperity and Self Worth." Then walk to number "five" and pause there briefly, breath deeply and exhale three times. Say a prayer of gratitude if you wish. Continue to number "six."

At number "six," visualize, accept, give thanks and release matters related to "Helpful People, Travel and Spirituality." Then walk to number "seven."

At number "seven" do the same for "Children, Creativity and Fun. "Walk to number "eight."

At number "eight" do the same for "Wisdom, Self-Knowledge and Stillness" Go to number "nine."

At number "nine" do the same for "Fame, Reputation and Social Life." Walk to number "one."

At number "one" do the same for "Career, Life Mission and Individuality." Then walk to number "2."

At number "two" do the same for "Relationships, Partnerships and Marriage." Then walk to the back door if there is one or go back to the front door. Before you leave, declare that you are done doing the cleanse and that all negativity in the room was either consumed by the fire or "trapped" in the feather.

Then walk to the back door, if there is one, or go back to the front door. Before you leave, declare that you are done with the blessing and that when you blow out the candle all the good intentions and your prayers remain in the room or building. Then exit.

Walk outside. If using a candle, let it burn out completely (please take all precautions); if using a feather wash it with abundant water (and soap if you wish).

At the center, if you wish, say 3 times: Thank you Dear God for my life, just as it is!

If you feel uncomfortable with the word God, substitute with the word that feels good to you, like: life, universe, great spirit, source, etc.

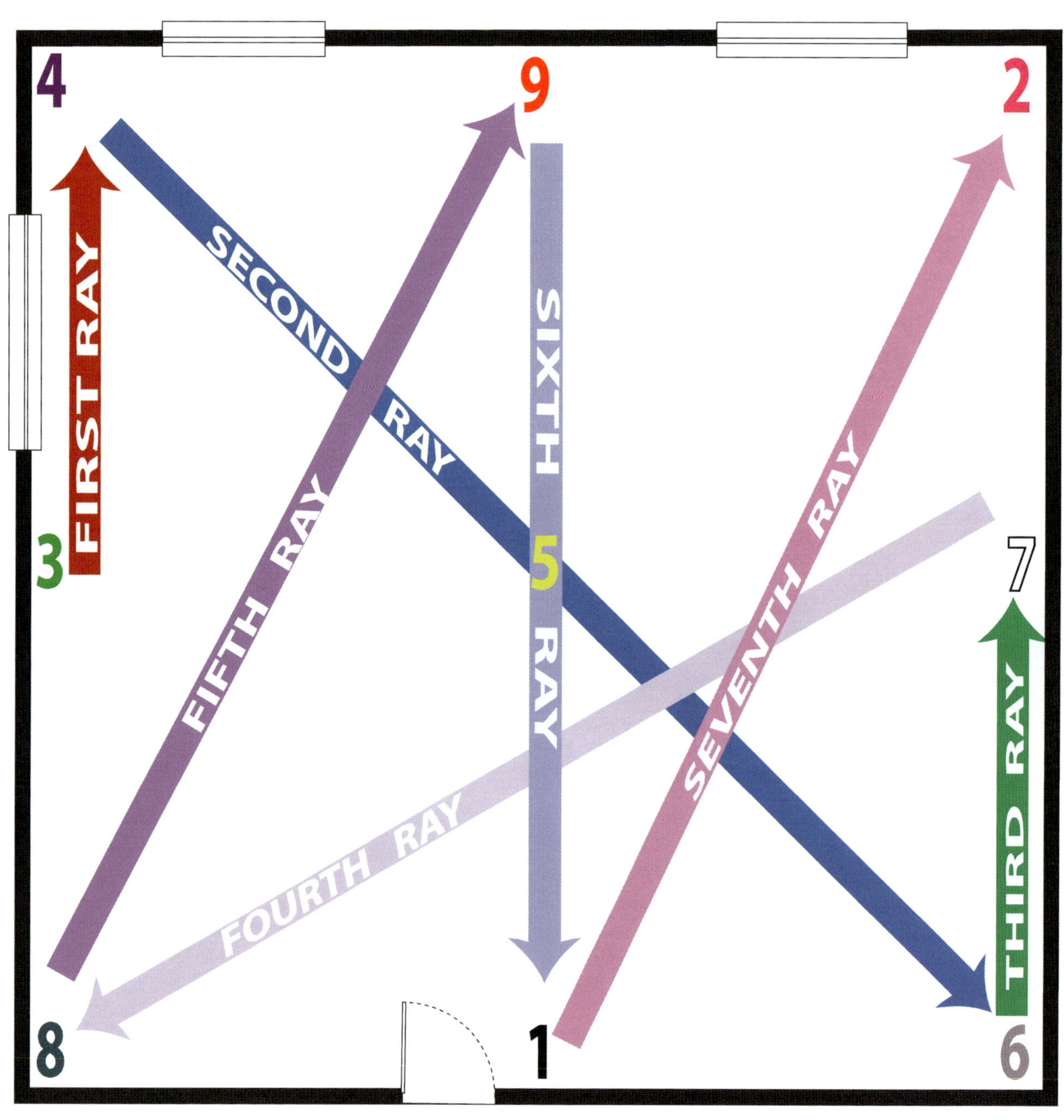

THE SEVEN ANGELIC RAYS ON THE FENG SHUI CLEARING PATTERN

THE SEVEN ANGELIC HEALING RAYS

The healing rays come from the Western Tradition of Alchemism.

There is no known connection between the meanings of the seven rays and the Life Aspirations. It is the pattern that their sequence creates when combined with the Magic Square that we use in the Nine Steps to Feng Shui® System.

First Ray:	Will or Power	Spiritual Red	Service	Walking from Health to (4) Wealth	1
Second Ray:	Love, Wisdom	Indigo	Expansion, Wisdom in Action	Walking from (4) Wealth, through the (5) Center, to (6) Helpful People	2
Third Ray:	Active Intelligence	Green	Clarity	Walking from (6) Helpful People to (7) Children	3
Fourth Ray:	Harmony, Beauty, Art	Violet and Moon Silver	Serenity	Walking from (7) Children directly to (8) Wisdom	4
Fifth Ray:	Science	Indigo-Violet	Direction	Walking from (8) Wisdom to (9) Fame	5
Sixth Ray:	Devotion, Idealism	Rose-Silver	Providence	Walking from (9) Fame to (1) Career	6
Seventh Ray:	Ceremonial Order	Violet	Ceremonial Order	Walking from (1) Career to (2) Marriage	7

Feng Shui for Us™

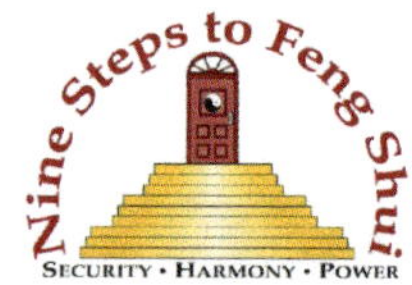

Nine Steps to Feng Shui
SECURITY • HARMONY • POWER

THE BA-GUA (LIFE AREAS) MAP ON THE MAGIC SQUARE

4 — WEALTH, PROSPERITY AND SELF-WORTH

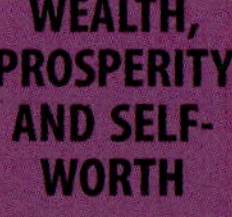

ELEMENT: WOOD

KEY WORDS/SYMBOLS: PENETRATION, PERSISTENCE, WORTH, DESERVING, HIP

TYPE OF CHI ENERGY: "The Gentle", Wind, Late Spring, 9am-12 Noon, Rising

COLORS: PURPLE, GREEN, GOLD

ENHANCE WITH: Healthy plants, images of material goals, small rocks and crystals, precious metals and stones, soft light sources, luxurious fabrics.

AVOID: Metallic objects, excessive white, red or fire symbols.

LOCATION:
Conscious: Kitchen
Unconscious: Left/Back Corner

9 — FAME, REPUTATION & SOCIAL LIFE

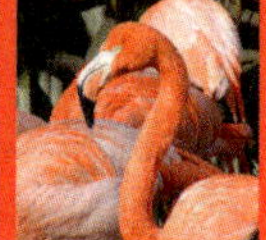

ELEMENT: FIRE

KEY WORDS: INTEGRITY, MAGNIFICENCE, PROPRIETY, EXPOSURE

TYPE OF CHI ENERGY: "The Clinging", Early Summer, 12 Noon-3pm, Radiating, Growth, Sun. **COLORS:** RED, BRIGHT ORANGE

ENHANCE WITH: Candles, lamps, images of people and animals, birds, the sun, symbols of achievement, awards.

AVOID: Water, colors blue and black, organic shapes, waves.

LOCATION: **Conscious:** Family Room.
Unconscious: Midsection of the Back Wall.

2 — MARRIAGE, RELATIONSHIPS AND PARTNERSHIPS

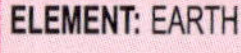

ELEMENT: EARTH

KEY WORDS/SYMBOLS: RECEPTIVITY, OBEDIENCE, YIELD, FAITH, WOMB

TYPE OF CHI ENERGY: "The Receptive", Earth, Late Summer, 3pm-6pm, Nourishment.

COLORS: PINK, SKIN & EARTH TONES.

ENHANCE WITH: Pairs: two doves, two swans, two roses, etc., images of loving couples, images of gardens, soft and sensual fabrics, cozy furniture.

AVOID: TV, religious images, family photos

LOCATION:
Conscious: Master Bedroom
Unconscious: Right/Back Corner

3 — HEALTH, FAMILY AND COMMUNITY

ELEMENT: WOOD

KEY WORDS/SYMBOLS: STRENGTH, PROGRESS, BENEVOLENCE, FOOT

TYPE OF CHI ENERGY: "The Arousing", Thunder, Early Spring, 6am-9am, Birth, Rising.

COLORS: ALL SHADES OF GREEN

ENHANCE WITH: Healthy plants, objects from nature, vertical stripes, images of nature, photos of family and friends.

AVOID: Metallic objects, excessive white, red or fire symbols.

LOCATION:
Conscious: Dining Room
Unconscious: Midsection of the Left Wall.

5 — GOOD FORTUNE CENTER

ELEMENT: EARTH

KEY WORDS: THANKFUL, CONFIDENT, TRUSTING

TYPE OF CHI ENERGY: Center, Axis, "Void"

ENHANCE WITH: Ceramic objects, religious symbols, images of agriculture and fruits, flowers.

COLORS: YELLOW, EARTH TONES

AVOID: Excess of metallic objects, plants.

LOCATION: Center of the building.

7 — CHILDREN, CREATIVITY & FUN

ELEMENT: METAL

KEY WORDS/SYMBOLS: JOY, INDULGENCE, CREATIVE FORCES, MOUTH

TYPE OF CHI ENERGY: "The Joyful," Lake, Early Fall, 6pm-9pm, Harvest, Winding Down.

COLORS: WHITE, AND PASTELS

ENHANCE WITH: Images of children, flowers, whimsical and colorful objects, artwork made by children, "casual" furniture

AVOID: Symbols of fire, water elements.

LOCATION:
Conscious: Children's Rooms, Art Studio. **Unconscious:** Midsection of the Right Wall.

8 — WISDOM, SELF-KNOWLEDGE AND REST

ELEMENT: EARTH

KEY WORDS/SYMBOLS: STILLNESS, PAUSE, COMPLETION, HALT, HAND

TYPE OF CHI ENERGY: "Keeping Still", Mountain, Late Winter, 3am-6am, Superficial Calm but Inner Activity.

COLORS: BLUE-GREEN

ENHANCE WITH: Images of mountains and quiet places, landscapes, books, comfortable seating, welcome mats.

AVOID: Artwork that is too active, plants and clocks.

LOCATION:
Conscious: Study, Home Library
Unconscious: Front/Left Corner.

1 — CAREER, LIFE MISSION & INDIVIDUALITY

ELEMENT: WATER

KEY WORDS/SYMBOLS: DEPTH, RISK, FALL, MOVING WATER, STORE, EAR

TYPE OF CHI ENERGY: "The Abysmal", Early Winter, 12 Midnight-3am, Water. **COLORS:** DARK BLUE, BLACK

ENHANCE WITH: Water fountains, aquariums, images of water or life in the water, especially streams and deep water, welcome mats, wind chimes.

AVOID: Excess of square shapes, ceramics, dryness.

LOCATION: **Conscious:** Foyer, Lobby, Hallways, Corridors
Unconscious: Midsection of the Front Wall.

6 — HELPFUL PEOPLE, SPIRITUAL LIFE & TRAVEL

ELEMENT: METAL

KEY WORDS/SYMBOLS: SYNCHRONICITY, RECTITUDE, HEAD

TYPE OF CHI ENERGY: "The Creator", Heaven, Sky, Late Fall, 9pm-12 Midnight, Preparation.

COLORS: GRAY, MAUVE

ENHANCE WITH: Religious symbols, angels, souvenirs from trips, images of places you would like to visit, photos of ancestors and teachers, welcome mats, wind chimes, soft light sources.

AVOID: Symbols of fire, water elements

LOCATION:
Conscious: Formal Living Room, Sanctuary, Altar
Unconscious: Front/Right Corner

www.fengshuiforus.com • (865) 973-1475

WALL THAT CONTAINS THE MAIN ENTRANCE

Declutter Your Own Spaces

Step

Help the Nine Life Areas by Addressing Types of Clutter

Feng Shui sees clutter as having the potential for creating stagnation for the nine life areas of the bagua map. Not all clutter is alike. Different types of clutter affect different life areas. Learn which these are, so you know what and where to declutter to free up energy in the life areas where you feel you have stagnated, or to alleviate worries or anxiety associated to a particular life area.

Feng Shui Your Own Life Areas

This is the book that goes over enhancing each life area, room by room.

STEP EIGHT: Help the Nine Life Areas by Addressing Types of Clutter

8.1 Decluttering with the Life Areas

Many times clients and students who are working on the Feng Shui of their life areas (step 8 in the Nine Steps to Feng Shui® System) find that even though they have applied the right cure for a life area, things are not improving at the pace that was expected. In cases like these, decluttering can be an invaluable tool to improve the life areas.

Decluttering the **corner** or **midpoint** that is associated with a life area can be very helpful, but there are also certain items around the home and certain places in the home that are in resonance with the different life areas.

Decluttering at the corner or midpoint can be very helpful, but when that is not enough, you may need to the declutter other spaces in the home that are associated with the nine life areas.

8.1.1 Life Area #1: Career, Life Mission and Individuality

To improve conditions in this life area, try decluttering:

- All periodicals: newspapers, magazines, and any other items you receive on a regular, cyclical basis.
- The foyer or lobby, hallways and staircases.

RELATIONSHIPS BETWEEN CLUTTER AND CORNERS/MIDPOINTS OF THE BUILDING, ROOMS IN THE HOME AND KINDS OF CLUTTER

4 WEALTH, PROSPERITY AND SELF-WORTH CLOTHING ITEMS (all things made of fabric) PERSONAL GROOMING CLOTHES CLOSETS	**9** FAME, REPUTATION & SOCIAL LIFE MEDIA: Audio cassettes, CDs, DVDs, Video cassettes, MAKEUP WALLS	MARRIAGE, RELATIONSHIPS AND PARTNERSHIPS **2** GIFTS, ORNAMENTS AND KNICKNACKS CURIO CABINETS BEDROOM DRAWERS
HEALTH, FAMILY AND COMMUNITY FOOD AND FOOD RELATED ITEMS **3** KITCHEN AND DINING DRAWERS AND CABINETS, BAGS	GOOD FORTUNE CENTER **5** MISCELLANEOUS, UNDEFINABLE ITEMS FLOORS	CHILDREN, CREATIVITY & FUN TOYS, ARTS AND CRAFTS SUPPLIES, HOBBY RELATED EQUIPMENT **7** CHESTS, BOXES MEDICINE CABINETS
WISDOM, SELF-KNOWLEDGE AND REST BOOKS SCHOOL SUPPLIES **8** BOOKCASES	CAREER, LIFE MISSION & INDIVIDUALITY PERIODICALS: Magazines, newspapers, newsletters, bulletins HALLWAYS, CORRIDORS, STAIRCASES **1**	HELPFUL PEOPLE, SPIRITUAL LIFE & TRAVEL PAPERWORK AND MAIL SOUVENIRS COUNTER TOPS AND TABLE TOPS **6**

WALL THAT CONTAINS THE FRONT ENTRANCE

Hold this chart at the door of a building or room to determine how the 9 areas of life are represented in your environment.

The entrance will always be through the areas with numbers 8, 1 or 6.

8.1.2 Life Area #2: Marriage, Relationships and Partnerships

To improve conditions in this life area, try decluttering:

- Gifts, ornaments and knick-knacks, curio cabinets.
- The master bedroom, especially night stand drawers and the top drawer(s) in dressers.

8.1.3 Life Area #3: Health, Family and Community

To improve conditions in this life area, try decluttering:

- Food and food-related items, such as plastic containers.
- Kitchen and dining drawers and cabinets.
- Bags (any types of bags you store).

8.1.4 Life Area #4: Wealth, Prosperity and Self-Worth

To improve conditions in this life area, try decluttering:

- Clothes and all other items made of fabric.
- Personal grooming items, such as creams, body washes, shampoos, etc.
- Clothes closets.

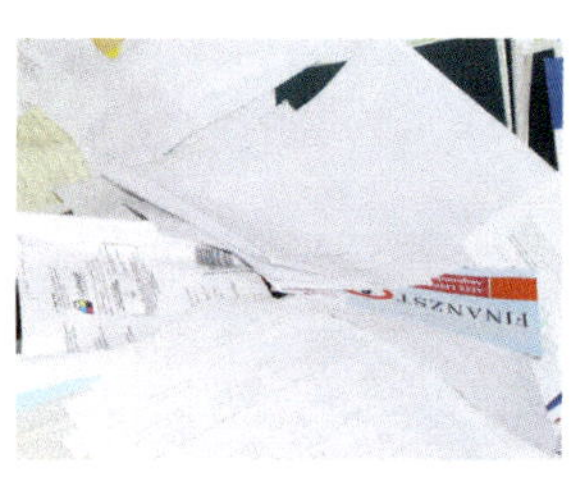

8.1.5 Life Area #5: Career, Life Mission and Individuality

To improve conditions in this life area, try decluttering:

- Miscellaneous items, those that are hard to define, or that keep being moved from one spot to another because you cannot quite decide what to do with them.
- Floors. Nothing that was not designed to be on the floor should be on the floor.

8.1.6 Life Area #6: Helpful People, Spiritual Life and Travel

To improve conditions in this life area, try decluttering:

- Paperwork and mail.
- Souvenirs.
- Horizontal surfaces other than the floor.

THE CLUTTER THAT HURTS A LIFE AREA THE MOST:

4 WEALTH, PROSPERITY AND SELF-WORTH KEEPING CLOTHES THAT DO NOT FIT RIGHT NOW [exception: pregnancy]	9 FAME, REPUTATION & SOCIAL LIFE KEEPING MOVIES OR MUSIC THAT LOWER YOUR ENERGY [make you feel bad]	MARRIAGE, RELATIONSHIPS AND PARTNERSHIPS 2 KEEPING GIFTS AND/ OR LETTERS FROM PREVIOUS LOVE RELATIONSHIPS
HEALTH, FAMILY AND COMMUNITY 3 FOOD THAT DECOMPOSES IN THE REFRIGERATOR, EXPIRED ITEMS IN THE PANTRY AND CABINETS	GOOD FORTUNE CENTER 5 HAVING STAGNANT CLUTTER ON THE FLOORS	CHILDREN, CREATIVITY & FUN KEEPING BROKEN TOYS OR SOUVENIRS, NO MATTER WHAT THE SENTIMENTAL 'VALUE' 7
WISDOM, SELF-KNOWLEDGE AND REST KEEPING BOOKS THAT DO NOT REFLECT WHO YOU ARE OR WHO YOU WANT TO BE 8	CAREER, LIFE MISSION & INDIVIDUALITY ACCUMULATING PERIODICALS TO 'READ ONE DAY' 1	HELPFUL PEOPLE, SPIRITUAL LIFE & TRAVEL FINANCIAL RECORDS IMPROPERLY KEPT 6

WALL THAT CONTAINS THE FRONT ENTRANCE

Hold this chart at the door of a building or room to determine how the 9 areas of life are represented in your environment.

The entrance will always be through the areas with numbers 8, 1 or 6.

VICES AND VIRTUES ON THE BAGUA MAP

4 WEALTH, PROSPERITY AND SELF-WORTH LAZINESS **DILIGENCE** ***PERFECT ACTION*** **Do what is right, be productive**	**9** FAME, REPUTATION & SOCIAL LIFE RAGE **PATIENCE** ***PERFECT EFFORT*** **Do today's work**	MARRIAGE, RELATIONSHIPS AND PARTNERSHIPS **2** STINGINESS **GENEROSITY** ***PERFECT VISION*** **See things as they are**
HEALTH, FAMILY AND COMMUNITY GLUTONY **3** **SELF CONTROL** ***PERFECT SURVIVAL*** **Have a constant dialogue with reality**	GOOD FORTUNE CENTER **5** CENTER, ***THE VOID, NO SIN*** **Be grateful**	CHILDREN, CREATIVITY & FUN LUST PURITY, INNOCENCE ***PERFECT ATTENTION*** **7** Be in the present
WISDOM, SELF-KNOWLEDGE AND REST ENVY/JEALOUSY **CHARITY** ***PERFECT FEELING*** **8** **Feel**	CAREER, LIFE MISSION & INDIVIDUALITY ARROGANCE **HUMILITY** ***PERFECT WORD*** **Tell the truth** **1**	HELPFUL PEOPLE, SPIRITUAL LIFE & TRAVEL HEAVEN, **CONTEMPLATION, PRAYER** ***ALREADY PERFECT NO SIN*** **Trust** **6**

WALL THAT CONTAINS THE FRONT ENTRANCE

Hold this chart at the door of a building or room to determine how the 9 areas of life are represented in your environment.

The entrance will always be through the areas with numbers 8, 1 or 6.

8.1.7 Life Area #7: Children, Creativity and Fun

To improve conditions in this life area, try decluttering:

- Toys, arts and crafts supplies, hobby items.
- Chests, trunks and boxes.
- Medicine cabinets.

8.1.8 Life Area #8: Wisdom, Self-Knowledge and Rest

To improve conditions in this life area, try decluttering:

- Books.
- School or college supplies.
- Bookcases.

8.1.9 Life Area #9: Fame, Reputation and Social Life

To improve conditions in this life area, try decluttering:

- Movies and music.
- Make up and parfumes or colognes.
- Walls and other vertical surfaces.

8.2 Decluttering Your Soul

Feng Shui considers that certain vices or bad habits tend to clutter the life areas, and conversely, that the cultivation of virtues and good habits unblocks the energy in the life areas and improves a person's performance in each of them.

Replace vices with virtues to declutter your soul!

On the graphic to the left of this page you can see a chart that correlates a vice and a virtue with each of the life areas.

You will also see the goal to which a person should aspire in each life area, in most cases preceded with the word "perfect." There is also a suggestion as to an action that can help clear and improve the energy of the life area in question.

For example, for Life Area #2, Marriage, Relationships and Partnerships, the vice is **stinginess**, the virtue is **generosity**, the aspiration is to have **perfect vision**, and the suggestion is to **see things as they are**.

8.3 Decluttering Prescriptions

Many Feng Shui books and practitioners tell you to "get rid of clutter." For most people, however, especially if they are dealing with organizational challenges, the task may seem overwhelming.

Decluttering prescriptions are recipes to clear clutter based on knowledge from Traditional Chinese Medicine. They usually consist of:

- a task, and
- a rhythm by which to perform that task

Decluttering prescriptions have been designed taking into account the type of clutter and the number that rules the Life Area to which it is related.

For example, clothing clutter is related to Life Area #4 (Wealth, Prosperity and Self Worth), so if you have reached a point where you feel your clothing clutter is out of control, especially if it is stagnant (closets full of clothes that haven't been used for a long time) your decluttering prescription will tell you to choose 4 garments that you either no longer use, don't love or that are torn. You would do this every 4 days and put them in a box or bag in the **Wealth, Prosperity and Self Worth Area** of your home and donate the box or bag of clothes after 4 weeks. If you wish, you may repeat the process however many times you feel you need to do it. Sometimes a person will find that after following the advice in a decluttering prescription they are able to continue the decluttering process at a much faster pace.

Please keep in mind that these are not general housekeeping and organizing tips, but rather advice on how to deal with certain kinds of items when we feel they have gotten out of hand. If you would like to learn more about acquiring good housekeeping habits, you may read the corresponding chapter for step 4 in this book.

8.3.1 PERIODICALS: Magazines, newspapers, newsletters, bulletins

This type of clutter affects Life Area #1 **Career, Life Mission and Individuality.** Classify your old periodicals by how often you received them (daily, weekly, monthly, quarterly, twice a year, yearly) and make piles with them. Start with the yearly, and twice a year publications, take a look at every item and decide if it is worth keeping, recycle at least two items a day until you are done. Then tackle quarterly and monthly publications and recycle at least four per day. When you get to weekly and daily publications, try to handle at least seven per day. You may want to get a couple of big 3-ring binders, scisors and a hole puncher, so that you can cut out pages with interesting articles and keep them tidy and organized. You may write the name and date of the publication on the top of the first page of each article. Alternatively, you can take digital photos of articles, to keep in your computer.

8.3.2 GIFTS, ORNAMENTS AND KNICKNACKS:

This kind of clutter is related to Life Area #2: **Marriage, Relationships and Partnerships.** This decluttering prescription has two stages:

STAGE ONE

First, look for all glass items that are broken or cracked and throw them out. No matter how much you like the item, once glass breaks or cracks, it cannot be fixed. Then, look for porcelain and ceramic items that are broken, cracked or chipped off. If they can be repaired so that the break won't be noticed, do it, if not, let them go.

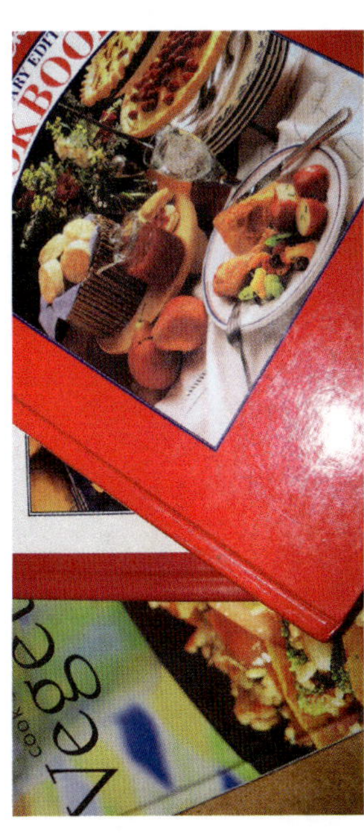

STAGE TWO

First, look for items that were given to you by people who no longer are in your life. Keep the ones that bring you good memories, let go of those that bring you bad memories, let go of **all** that were given to you by a former romantic partner. Then, look for items that even though they were given to you by people who love you, either don't go with your style or you simply don't like them, and let them go. If it makes you feel better, first talk to the person who gave them to you and explain that you are in a decluttering process and ask if they wouldn't mind if you donated the item they gave you to a charity, while reassuring them of your love.

Keep only those gifts, ornaments and knicknacks that are in good condition and that you LOVE. Objects have a life span too, let your loved objects of the past have an honorable passing, rather than letting them deteriorate until they no longer resemble their former beauty.

8.3.3 FOOD AND FOOD-RELATED ITEMS

This kind of clutter is related to Life Area #3: **Health, Family and Community.**

Every three days take a look at the provisions in your cabinets, pantry and refrigerator and find three items that have either expired (in which case you need to throw them out) or that are about to expire (in which case you may use them to plan your next meal or meals). Do this for three weeks.

8.3.4 CLOTHING ITEMS:

Clothing clutter is related to Life Area #4 **Wealth, Prosperity and Self Worth**, so if you have reached a point where you feel your clothing clutter is out of control, especially if it is stagnant (closets full of clothes that haven't been used for a long time): Choose 4 garments that you either no longer use, don't love or that are torn. You would do this every 4 days and put them in a box or bag in the Wealth, Prosperity and Self Worth Area of your home and donate the box or bag of clothes after 4 weeks.

If you wish, you may repeat the process however many times you feel you need to do it.

8.3.5 MISCELLANEOUS, UNDEFINABLE ITEMS

For five months, on the fifth Sunday [or choose another day] of the month, identify:

1. Five items that you don't even know what they are.
2. Five business cards, brochures or sticky notes with phone numbers that you do not know who they belong to.
3. Five items that do not belong to any member of your household.
4. Five items that are parts or pieces or manuals of greater objects that are no longer in your home.
5. Five oddities (or whatever else you would define as miscellaneous).

Have a meeting with your family members or co-workers to make sure none of the identified items belong or can be of use to anybody present. Then recycle, throw away or donate what is left.

8.3.6 PAPERWORK AND MAIL

Paperwork:

To tackle big piles of paper that have been accumulated for a long time:

Every six days choose from your stack:

1. Six items that are junk and can be put away in the recycling bin.

2. Six items that you would like to keep but don't actually need to keep and place them in a filing box or accordion file marked accordingly.

3. Six items that can be filed and don't require any further action on your part, place them in a filing box or accordion file marked accordingly.

4. Six items that require an action on your part and place them in the appropriate folders of your temporary file (see below).

Then:

5. Every six weeks go through the three filing boxes you created above and decide whether to recycle, take action and file or keep the items in the box.

6. Consider upgrading to a permanent filing system that is big enough to take care of your filing needs.

Taking Care of Mail:

Separate the daily mail into four stacks: window envelopes, regular envelopes, mailers with no envelope, and packages.

- Window envelopes are usually sent to you by businesses,solicited or unsolicited. First, separate the outer envelope from the mail and (hopefully) recycle the envelopes. (Many cities in the US now allow window envelopes to be recycled without requiring that the plastic be removed, check with the recycling program in your town). This reduces your pile to close to half. You don't need to keep the outer envelope because their communications will have their address and possibly a return envelope with their address. If it is junk mail, tear it up or shred it and then place it in your recycling bin. If it is real business mail, recycle all advertising materials enclosed in the package and keep only that which requires an action on your part (e.g. payment or filing) and the return envelope if necessary (if you make your payments online there is no need to keep that envelope!)

- Regular envelopes. Open up these envelopes in order to determine if they are real mail or junk mail. If they are junk mail go ahead and tear up/shred and recycle the envelope and its contents. If it is real mail and it doesn't come with a return envelope, check to see if you already have this person's or this business' address in your records. If you don't, keep the envelope until you get a chance to record the return address, otherwise place the envelope in the recycling bin. Keep only that which requires an action on your part (e.g. payment or filing) and the return envelope if necessary (if you make your payments online there is no need to keep that envelope!) Place greeting cards in a special "gratitude bag" to be recycled at the end of the year. If it's a greeting you want to keep for a long time, place it in a special file.

- Mailers with no envelope. Place those you have no interest in the recycle bin. Keep only those you want to read or are announcements for some upcoming event.

In addition to your regular filing system (you have one, don't you?) get a temporary filing gadget that keeps paper vertical in separate slots instead of an in-basket. Create at list these folders:

- Bills to Pay (check this one daily)

- Bills Paid (to file)

- Need to file

- Events I might attend

- Events I have attended

- Movies I might watch

- Possible purchases

- and any other subjects that characterize mail you get often and don't want to let go of right away but wouldn't necessarily file away in a permanent file.

- Packages that come to you are usually things you have ordered: get the product out, trash, reuse or recycle all packaging materials right away and place user manuals in the "Need to file" folder of your temporary file.

Reduce Mail, Email and Phone Calls

You can greatly reduce the amount of work and the time it takes to sort through mail and email every day by **opting out** of mailing and emailing lists. There are several organizations you can find online (search for "do not mail") that can help you achieve this.

I have successfully used **www.dmachoice.org** to dramatically reduce the amount of "snail mail" we receive each day. They also have an option to opt out of emailing lists. If you live in the United States, you can go to **www.donotcall.gov** to enter your phone numbers in the "Do Not Call" list to prevent telemarketers from adding your numbers to their calling lists.

8.3.7 TOYS, ARTS AND CRAFTS SUPPLIES, HOBBY RELATED EQUIPMENT

Toys **belong to the children** to whom they were given as presents. It is OK to make decisions for children three years old or younger, but for children over that age, you will need to have their **consent** and cooperation for decluttering when it comes to their toys. One way you may achieve this, is by setting the rule that a trip to the toy store is always preceded by a trip to the thrift store to donate toys they don't play with any more. If there are too many toys in your home, for a while you may allow your children only one new toy for every two or three that are donated.

If your house has been taken over by toys and you are dealing with a major need for decluttering, you may use this recipe:

- Let go of any toys that resemble people or animals that are missing body parts.

- Let go of any puzzles that are missing pieces.

- Let go of any toys that are missing pieces if they are inoperable as a consequence (for example a shape sorter with no pieces to fit in the holes).

- Let go of any odd items, for example single doll shoes, or a hat that doesn't fit any doll.

- Let go of any toys that your child has outgrown for over a year, with the exception of a few loved toys that are worth keeping for memories sake.

If you decide to have a yard or garage sale, keep in mind that any money that comes from sale of toys should go to their rightful owners – the

children, either to spend themselves, put in a savings account, or for parents to purchase things their children need.

8.3.8 BOOKS, SCHOOL SUPPLIES

Let go of eight books per week and do this eight weeks in a row. To choose which books to let go of, ask yourself these questions:

- Will I ever read this book again?
- Will I ever use this book to look for references?
- Is this book an heirloom?

If you answered "no" to ALL three questions, then this book does not belong in your space any more. If you answered "yes" to any of them, then keep it.

If you visited someone you just met at their home, you would form an opinion about their lives, their beliefs, and their moral values, based on the books they keep.

You also make a judgement on yourself at home, based on the reading materials you keep. You could say that your books ***define*** you. Make sure your books are telling the story of who you truly are and who you desire to be.

8.3.9 MEDIA: Audio cassettes, CDs, DVDs, Video cassettes

Every nine days, choose one type of media to declutter. Then ask yourself:

- Do I still like this music or movie?
- Does this kind of music or movie still reflect who I am and who I want to be?
- Will I ever watch this movie again? Do I ever listen to this music?

If you answered "no" to ANY of the above questions, then let go of that item.

Declutter Your Own Spaces

Step

The Power of Pre-Deciding and Using Systems

Many people find that even though they are able to keep their spaces tidy and organized at work, things at home get out of control. This happens because at work we have systems set up. These systems are based on rules and rules are pre-decisions that we make so that we do not have to ponder what to do about things every time.

STEP NINE: Pre-Decide and Use Systems

9.1 Pre-Decide

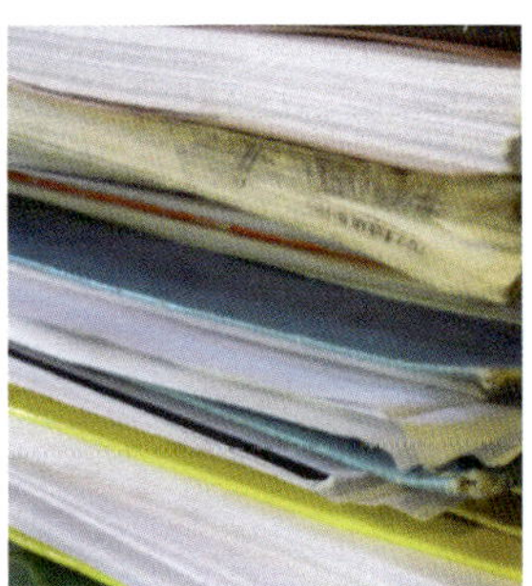

It is a lot easier to organize paper if it is kept vertical, instead of in piles.

Pre-decisions are rules about what to do every time when similar situations arise. They save time and brain power.

9.1.1 Pre-Decide What to Do with Paper

Take care of your mail every day. Throw away or recycle junk mail without opening it. Even better, do not even let junk mail cross the threshold of your home. If you can't resist taking a peek at it, keep two incoming baskets: one for real mail and another one for junk mail, and empty out the second one at least once a week. The first basket will hold mainly letters, postcards, etc. that need to be answered, and bills that need to be paid (but that you are not necessarily going to pay right away).

Make sure you have a place to *temporarily* store newspapers and magazines you have subscribed to and catalogs you might order from in the future, or otherwise they will be laying around the house creating clutter. Unless you collect them, donate all magazines at least once a year, but ideally with each change of season (every three months).

Once a year, go through your book shelves and sell or give away those you feel no longer belong in your collection (the internet now provides wonderful sites where you can buy and sell second hand books).

9.1.2 Pre-Decide How to Handle Recycling

Do not make your concern for the environment an excuse to live in a messy place. Many people who have trouble letting go of things they do not need, including what is obviously garbage, plan to recycle and then procrastinate so that they get to keep the junk for months after it should have been disposed of. If you mean to recycle be serious and organized about it. Get adequate containers, preferably with lids, where you can sort out and neatly keep glass bottles, plastic items, aluminum products and paper until they are picked up or dropped off. Do not wait until the container is full, let your recyclables be picked up or drop them off based on a weekly, bi-weekly or monthly schedule.

The concern for the cleanliness of the planet starts at home. If a person claims to be an activist for planetary ecology, but doesn't care to help clean his or her own city, would you take that person seriously? If a person claimed to be concerned for the environment in their community, but did not take care of their own yard, would you believe them?

The preservation of Earth's ecology starts at home, in our storage rooms, closets and drawers. Moreover, it starts at the stores, when we refrain from buying items that we do not need or love, as they will most likely become trash, whether we keep them at home or throw them away.

Organizing Paper

Paper is only orderly when kept vertical,

any attempt to organize paper horizontally

will produce clutter

9.1.3 Pre-Decide What Not to Buy

Do not buy things you do not need. If you feel the impulse to acquire them, try this strategy: load them in the shopping cart or carry them around until you are ready to check out. This will often calm the urge to buy them and you will feel OK about returning them to their shelves (don't just drop them anywhere, please).

Every Spring and Fall, engage your family members in a general cleanse, and get rid of the things that are trash and those that you do not need, do not use, do not love, or that bring you bad memories.

9.1.4 Pre-Decide How to Handle Laundry

The first step in managing your laundry is learning to keep an inventory of your clothes.

At the end of every season, look through the clothes you have worn during the last three months and remove from your closet all items that:

- look too old
- are torn and cannot be mended
- do not fit anymore
- are outdated
- you will not wear the next year
- have colors that do not become you

- do not look good on you
- are uncomfortable to wear
- you do not love

Throw away those that cannot be worn any more, or use them for cleaning rags) and donate the rest to your local charity second hand shop, or give them away to people you know who might appreciate them.

Then put away the clothes that you want to keep but will not be wearing during the upcoming season(s).

Make sure to leave some breathing room in closets and drawers. When these are too full and you have to struggle to get items out it becomes much easier to disorganize the rest.

Some households that have an actual laundry room can keep baskets and/or bags there to sort out different kinds of clothing. When there is no laundry room but just a laundry closet, the laundry bags or baskets are kept either in the bathroom or in individual rooms. Parents having trouble getting their children to pick up their dirty clothes and take them to either the bathroom or laundry room may find that placing laundry bags or baskets in the child's room may be an adequate compromise. It will prevent having dirty clothes just laying on the floor.

Store the following items separately, either in different pieces of furniture, cabinets or drawers, and also wash them separately:

- clothes
- bathroom towels and robes
- sheets, pillowcases
- bed covers, throws
- tablecloths, kitchen linens and towels

Follow the manufacturers' instructions, especially when washing new items, as some may discolor during the first wash. It is better to wash new items by themselves the first time unless you are sure they will not stain other pieces of clothing. Soaking hand-dyed items in cold water with salt for a couple of hours before the first wash will help set the colors. If you have to adjust the hem of pants or skirts, wash and dry them once before you do it, as they might shrink.

A woman I knew once said: "I would rather have a big pile of dirty clothes than a big pile of wrinkled clothes." I agree. Remove clothes from the dryer as soon as the cycle is complete and either hang or fold them. If you have enough hanging space in your closet, you may find that hanging T-shirts works better and is faster than folding them and putting them away in drawers. Hang clothes that need ironing if you can't get to them right away, rather than piling them up. This will make ironing easier.

A friend of mine who has four children, gets the clothes out of the dryer and "pre-folds" them and places them on piles on each child's bed and then they take care of putting them away. This works great for them.

If you buy clothes at a second hand shop, be aware that the personal Chi of the previous owner may still be impregnated in the item(s). Turning them inside out and hanging them outdoors under the sun will help clear their energy from the pieces of clothing. You can also soak them in cold salt water for two hours and then rinse them out, if the material allows it. For material or fabrics that cannot be soaked, you can either spray them on the inside with a very penetrating and invigorating aroma like peppermint, eucalyptus or ginger (if you know the material won't be damaged), or burn oil or incense with these kind of aromas and expose the item(s) to the vapors.

9.1.5 Pre-Decide What to Do with Those Undefinable Objects

After paper and laundry, undefinable objects are the third source of clutter in a home or office. These are all those little items that we never seem to find a place for, we do not know if we should keep them, who they belong to or how they got there. Keep a tray or small basket to be your home or workplace "lost and found" department, where you can place all of these objects and once a week invite your house mates to look through it and decide what to do about them.

9.1.6 Pre-Decide How to Keep a Car Tidy

There are three items that can be very helpful when it comes to keeping a car tidy:

- A trash bag. This can be as simple as a paper or plastic bag, or as elegant as a leather bag lined up with a paper or plastic bag that you can attach to the dashboard.

- A backpack to hang from the passenger front seat or a small plastic container to hold items that you might need while in the car, but that do not need to stay in the car at all times. When you get home or to your workplace you can carry it with you. Use the glove compartment only for items that stay permanently in the car and do not over stuff it.

- One or two big plastic containers to keep in the trunk. This way. If you purchase potting soil or any frozen goods, you know that any spills will be limited to the inside of the box, which you can easily remove and wash if necessary.

9.1.7 Pre-Decide to Keep Storage Areas Organized

In any storage room at any time we should be able to walk in, look around and at a glance locate the item(s) we are looking for. You know you have problems if a storage room is so full you cannot walk in. The secret to good storage is:

KEEP NOTHING ON THE FLOOR

Every single item should be on a shelf, inside a drawer, inside plastic boxes (even if they are stacked on top of one another), on shelves, or hanging from hooks. The more you label, the less time you will waste looking for things.

There are plenty of plastic and wire accessories that you can use to maximize closet and cabinet space. Take advantage of them.

9.1.8 Pre-Decide to Keep Tidy

If when doing your routine cleaning and organizing you ever feel overwhelmed do the following: stand in the middle of the room, look around you and identify, among all that needs cleaning/organizing, what bothers you the most. This is usually the item or pending chore that holds a great deal of your attention and therefore drains your energy. Once that issue is resolved you will free up enough energy to continue on to the next troublesome issue, and so forth.

9.2 Dusting, Sweeping and Vacuuming

The purpose of dusting is to remove dust from pieces of furniture and fixtures. Make sure that your duster is able to pick up the dust, not just redistribute it in the air so that it will fall on the furniture or on the carpet. Dusting can be done "dry," with feather or synthetic fiber dusters, or "wet" with a proper spray and paper towels or rags. What you use depends on your personal preference and the material of the items you are cleaning. Use regular bottle sprays rather than aerosols, they are better for the environment and for your own health. Diluted Castile soap is one of the safest and most effective cleaning agents for the household, you can use it on any smooth surface except wood.

Household dust is made up mostly of dead skin cells that people and pets shed and lint from paper and clothing. Microscopic critters feed on the particles of dust. If we do not clean, these "natural cleaners" multiply. When people are exposed to them they can develop rashes, colds or allergies. Do not get used to living with household dust. It carries the energy of death and it attracts bad energies into the home or office.

Choose a vacuum cleaner that does not throw dust back into your space –what is the point of vacuuming then? There are new models today that do not work with bags and have better filtering mechanisms. They are especially recommended for people with allergies or respiratory problems. I believe everybody has the right to breath cleaner air in their own homes.

Lift from the floor any objects that might get in your way in every room **before** you enter with the vacuum cleaner. Only furniture, rugs and some light fixtures should be on the floor at any time. All other objects should be on top of furniture, on shelves, inside cabinets or drawers, or hanging from hooks. Otherwise, they become land mines waiting to explode whenever somebody steps on them or kicks them.

I never cease to be amazed at how very few people have actually learned how to sweep without sending clouds of dust in all directions. When sweeping, extend the broom away from you and then softly drag the dirt in your direction (slightly in front of you). Most people start with the broom right next to them and then push it away from them, making the ends of the broom's fibers snap like tiny bows, which throws dust back into the space (check out the figure on the right side of this page).

A swinging broom movement disperses dust back into the environment

Start by placing the broom away from you and then drag the dust and debris towards you with a horizontal motion.

Odors

People get used to odors pretty quickly and during consultations I have found that more often than not, when there are strong disagreeable smells in the home or office, the people who live or work there are unaware of them. This is especially true of musty smells from dampness, smells from food, and smells from pets.

It is a good practice to keep some source of good scent in our spaces at all times, as in candles (whether you light them or not), potpourri, essential oils, etc., especially near the entrance. Choosing natural products is best.

For strong smells like those of pets, you may try commercial sprays or powders, or air filters and purifiers. Many air cleaning devices have filters made of charcoal, as this is a natural odor absorber. It helps to place a paper bag of charcoal inside a closet, cabinet or basement corner with very strong and persistent bad smell, and replace it every two weeks until it clears. Odor absorbing rocks are also sold in the market. When they get saturated with smells, you can leave them under the sun for a few hours to reactivate and reuse them.

I have found air purifiers that release ions and ozone are effective odor controllers. There are some concerns – and not complete agreement – about potential negative effects of ozone on people and pets and about magnetic fields generated by ionic purifiers. If you are dealing with some kind of odor that nothing short of this kind of device will control, a good alternative is to turn it on when you are going out and turn it off when you come home.

Of course, bad smells are much easier to combat when a place is kept clean, and impossible to get rid of when kept dirty.

9.3 Invite some Workplace Systems into the Household

The main difference between activities in the workplace and at home is that at the office or at the shop we feel more pressure to get things done. This pressure forces us to be more organized and to leave fewer things undone. Because we usually work with other people, it becomes very important that anybody in the workplace be able to find the right tools and papers and that every one knows what is expected of them. I believe that three business practices as related to the space can be very helpful when managing a household: labeling, filing and job descriptions.

9.3.1 Labeling

The most organized workplaces are those that provide a place for each item and where closets, cabinets, drawers and even hooks on the wall are clearly visible and labeled. Invite this practice into your home.

Except the people who do the cooking, most family members do not really know where things are stored in the kitchen. So is it any wonder that when un-stacking the dishwasher items end up in the most unexpected places?

Likewise, the people with whom you live with may not be aware of where the scissors are to be kept or they may forget about them if they do not use them often.

Labeling will help everybody know where things go, where to put them away and where to find them, without straining their memory.

Even if you live by yourself, labeling will free up your time and mental energy.

This can be done very discreetly, on inside shelves or behind cabinet doors, or very boldly. That is your choice. It can be done with actual words, drawings, or clippings, or even wood ornaments or painted tiles. You can be very practical or very creative. You can use color coding.

9.3.2 Filing

Replace those shoe boxes, tin boxes, binders, and bagfuls of paper with an actual filing system. You can find them in many different sizes and varieties. The most economical are made of plastic and may be limited to one drawer with a lid. The ones we see more often are made of metal and have two to five drawers. Some are wooden and beautifully crafted to match furniture sets.

These are some items that you might consider keeping in separate folders in your filing system:

- manuals from household appliances and devices
- one for each bank account
- miscellaneous reading materials (this includes articles from magazines or newspapers that you might read some time, instead of keeping the whole publication, just cut out the article)
- school documents, one folder per person
- personal, official and medical documents, one per person in the household (i.e. birth and marriage certificates, hospital records, etc.)
- one folder per car in the household, to keep the title, registration, insurance records, receipts for car tags and service records
- one folder per property owned or rented, to keep deeds, contracts, floor plans, surveys, insurance records, receipts for repairs or improvements done, etc.
- one for each of the following house expenses: electricity, gas, water and sewer, phone service, internet service provider and cable (or satellite), or, if you prefer, just keep one folder for all of them and call it "utilities"
- receipts you need for tax deductions, by category
- old miscellaneous invoices, bills and receipts, by month
- correspondence and greeting cards you need or want to keep
- pet records
- catalogs
- internet printouts
- miscellaneous

Keep some blank labels and folders inside the filing cabinet, so that they will always be easily available.

Keep the headings on the folders short and as simple as possible, like: "Mike," "Pets," "Truck," "Phone," etc.

At home, it is better to file by categories rather than by date, but in each folder, put the latest items in front, so that they will be in chronological order, from newest to oldest.

9.3.5 Shoe Racks

There is no better way to keep shoes organized than the way they are organized at shoe stores.

If you have a walking closet, you can get a shoe rack that can be fixed to the wall.

If you have a built in closet, you can get a shoe rack that hangs from the pole.

Another option for organizing shoes is to get an over-the-door rack, but this works only with the kind that have pockets for each shoe, because they are not too deep and therefore do not impede opening the door. **Do not** use an over the door shoe rack if it makes it hard to open the door to 90 degrees.

9.3.3 Bulletin boards

These are a great idea. Every home or office should have an area where anybody can post messages for the other family members or coworkers. Just make sure to keep yours up to date. I have found bulletin boards filled with messages that were several months old while sticky notes are overflowing and filling up the walls around them.

9.3.4 Job Descriptions

When a person has grown up performing certain house chores, it may not occur to him or her that his or her house mates may not even have a clue about how to go about them, or that they may be doing them in different ways or even doing them the wrong ways. You do not have to write down what is involved in each house chore, though you may if you wish to, but make sure that when a person has been asked to help with a certain task that he or she actually knows how to do it properly.

For example, in one household, the task of taking out the trash may be limited to dragging the big trash can out to the curb, while in another one it may involve walking through the house emptying out the smaller trash cans, replacing the old plastic bags with new ones, and returning the big trash can to its place after the city truck has emptied it out. Make sure each person living in your home knows what chores they are expected to perform, that they know what each of those entail, and that they know how to do them properly.

If it helps, imagine that you are a hotel manager, teaching the staff how to perform chores.

9.3.6 Scheduling

Along with job descriptions, scheduling can be immensely helpful in organizing a home so that in produces the minimum amount of clutter in the future. In your job descriptions you assigned tasks to individuals. It is important that those individuals know, preferable in writing, what is the frequency with which they are expected to perform those tasks.

On pages 124 and 125 you will see some charts that list a number of household chores. One of the charts is meant for you and your family to decide the frequency with which you desire that these chores be done. The other chart provides space to write down the name of the person responsible for the task.

9.3.7 Chores Assignations Based on Knowledge, Ability and Preference

Just like in a work environment you would have requirements in terms of education, knowledge and experience in order to assign jobs to employees, at home you should consider your family members' abilities and inclinations when assigning tasks.

For example, for years it had been my job to vacuum the carpet in our home, and it had been my husband's job to take the recyclables to the plant. However, in a recent conversation, my husband admitted that he "hated" taking care of the recyclables. Since I do not particularly care for vacuuming, I suggested that he be responsible for vacuuming, which he does not mind, while I would be responsible for taking items to the recycling plant, which is something I actually like to do.

Look at the form to the right of this page. Make copies of it and distribute to each family member. Use the results to try and assign chores that will not feel overwhelming to each family member.

What family members like to do or not in terms of household jobs, and what areas of the home they are avoiding, can give you important clues as to what is going on in their life areas.

HOUSEHOLD CHORES

RESPONSIBILITIES

KITCHEN AND DINING	
COOKING	
DOING DISHES	
WASHING POTS & PANS	
WIPING DOWN COUNTERS	
CLEANING DINING TABLE	
SWEEPING	
MOPING	
CLEANING REFRIGERATOR	
EMPTYING OUT & CLEANING CABINETS	
EMPTYING OUT & CLEANING PANTRY	
BATHROOMS	
CLEANING COUNTER & SINK	
WIPING MIRRORS	
CLEANING THE TOILET	
SCRUBBING THE SHOWER	
SCRUBBING THE TUB	
MOPPING THE FLOOR	
WASHING SHOWER CURTAIN OR DOOR	
BEDROOMS, LIVING, HALLWAYS	
MAKING THE BED	
PICKING UP	
DUSTING	
VACUUMING FLOORS	
VACUUMING FURNITURE	
LAUNDRY	
CLOTHING	
LINENS	
TOWELS	
BLANKETS AND BEDCOVERS	
WINDOW TREATMENTS	
IRON	
PETS	
WALK THE DOG	
CLEAN CAT LITTER	
BRUSHING	
CLEAN AQUARIUM	
CLEAN CAGE	
OTHER	
SWEEP PATIO	
WIPE DOWN OUTDOOR FURNITURE	
SWEEP GARAGE	
YARD WORK (MOW, RAKE, SHOVEL)	
DOING WINDOWS	
CLEANING LIGHT FIXTURES	
ATTIC	
BASEMENT	
STORAGE ROOM OR SHED	

Declutter Your Own Spaces

Appendix

APPENDIX

In the following pages you will find a chart and three forms that may be useful to you as you learn to deal with clutter and organize your home or business

Page 128

Many people insist that they like clutter and they simply feel more at ease and comfortable in a cluttered space. This usually shows the person has become numb to the clutter. Remember that in Feng Shui we don't mind messes as much as stagnation, when things have been messy for a while. Consider what constitutes clutter in the human body: growths, cysts, tumors, polyps, stones – when things that should leave the body or leave the space, instead stay, the results threaten health and happiness.

Page 129

On page 129 you will find a sample sheet for creating job descriptions at home, or even for your small business.

Page 130

Many people these days use their phones, tablets or computers to keep their "To-Do" lists. Nevertheless, sometimes it may feel really refreshing to write down the most important things that need to be done in a day and then cross them out as you complete them. You can copy these forms on the back of copy or print paper that you have already used, to save paper and trees.

Page 131

One challenge that clients report in keeping filing cabinets in order is that **they forget** how they labeled file folders. For example, when filing documents pertaining to the water and sewer bills, a client might create one folder called "Water/Sewer" and put some bills in there, and then later on forget there is already a folder for these and create another called "Sewer/Water," or even another folder labeled with the name of the water service company. For this reason it is very helpful to keep a record of the file folders you have labeled.

CLUTTER IN THE BODY, BY LIFE AREA & HELPFUL STATES OF BEING

4 WEALTH, PROSPERITY AND SELF-WORTH **FATTY DEPOSITS IN THE LIVER** ***Be Industrious***	**9** FAME, REPUTATION & SOCIAL LIFE **ARTERIAL PLAQUE** ***Be Honest***	MARRIAGE, RELATIONSHIPS AND PARTNERSHIPS **2** **UTERINE FIBROMAS ENDOMETRIOSIS** ***Be Generous***
HEALTH, FAMILY AND COMMUNITY **3** **GALLBLADDER STONES** ***Be Caring***	GOOD FORTUNE CENTER **5** **STOMACH NODULES** ***Be Grateful***	CHILDREN, CREATIVITY & FUN **PULMONARY FIBROSIS** **7** Be Playful
WISDOM, SELF-KNOWLEDGE AND REST **EXCESS FAT** **8** ***Be Humble***	CAREER, LIFE MISSION & INDIVIDUALITY **KIDNEY STONES** ***Be Responsible*** **1**	HELPFUL PEOPLE, SPIRITUAL LIFE & TRAVEL **COLON POLYPS** ***Be Timely*** **6**

WALL THAT CONTAINS THE FRONT ENTRANCE

Hold this chart at the door of a building or room to determine how the 9 areas of life are represented in your environment.

The entrance will always be through the areas with numbers 8, 1 or 6.

HOUSEHOLD CHORES

JOB DESCRIPTIONS

NAME OF THE CHORE ____________________

FREQUENCY ____________________

PERSON RESPONSIBLE ____________________

TOOLS REQUIRED ____________________

PROCEDURE: ____________________

DESIRED END RESULT ____________________

PENDING CHORES

DATE

PRIORITY
Use a pencil

✔ Done
✖ Undone
➔ Pending

FILE FOLDERS RECORD

Letter Under Which it was Filed	File Folder Name	YEAR IT WAS CREATED	Letter Under Which it was Filed	File Folder Name	YEAR IT WAS CREATED

I hope you have enjoyed reading this book and that you are already implementing some of the life-changing tools I have shared with you.

I look forward to hearing of your successes as you use this system.

You may review this book on Amazon.com and/or contact me at :
moni@fengshuiforus.com

When you have experienced the blessings of tranquility and harmony in your home as a result of your application of the knowledge in this text and are ready for more, consider the texts on page 134 to continue your journey down the path of a loving life with Feng Shui.

And if you yearn for an even deeper understanding of Feng Shui, please consider taking the Nine Steps to Feng Shui® Online Course.

Please visit my website www.fengshuiforus.com

Many Blessings,

Moni

Change:

"I am so confused."

Into:

"I understand Feng Shui now!"

Before they start their studies with me, most students tell me that they are confused. They have tried to apply Feng Shui on their own, but got stuck with some question, or their cures did not produce the expected results.

After they take the Nine Steps to Feng Shui® Online Course this is what they say:

The Nine Steps to Feng Shui® Online Course makes small changes. It also explains concepts that I never learned from other Feng Shui books or practitioners, so the small changes have a big impact.

I wholeheartedly endorse the Nine Steps to Feng Shui® Online Course for anyone that wants to gain a greater understanding of a complex and fascinating art.

Lynda Concord, Knoxville, TN

Thank you so much for offering your Nine Steps to Feng Shui® Online Course. It is so much easier to learn about Feng Shui and work on the things I have learned, one step at a time. I am so grateful that I found your site. You make it simple and easy to understand. I like being able to review the prior videos as well.

Robin R., Montana

The content was very informative and easy to understand. I feel that I can go into a home or business and practice the Nine Steps System with ease and grace.

Moni was a great instructor, being a teacher myself I know the importance of conveying information in an effective way and not making the student feel "silly" for asking a question. Moni answered all of my questions quickly and she made me feel excited about Feng Shui.

The videos were clear and detailed and were posted in a timely manner so that the course "flowed" and there weren't any interruptions because you could refer back to the manuals and charts that were included in the course. I have previously read many books about feng shui but I was always confused about doing it as a profession because of the conflicting information out there.

Moni brings a fresh perspective that is both holistic and healing and she teaches it from a love paradigm which is absolutely awesome!

Tatia Biddle, Milwaukee, WI

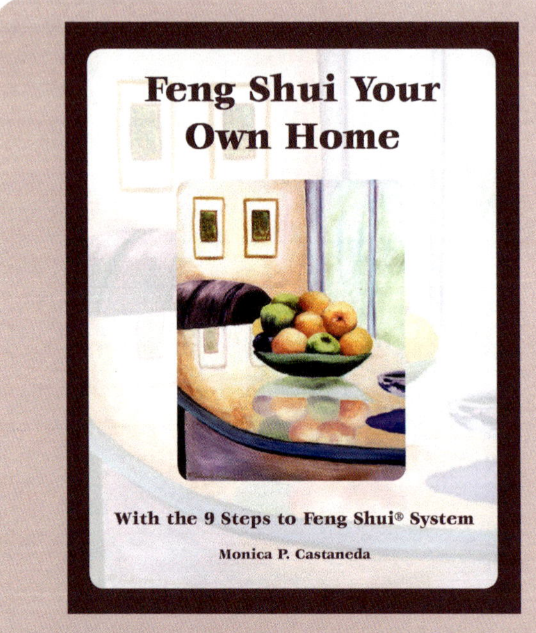

Feng Shui Your Own Home
with the 9 Steps to Feng Shui® System

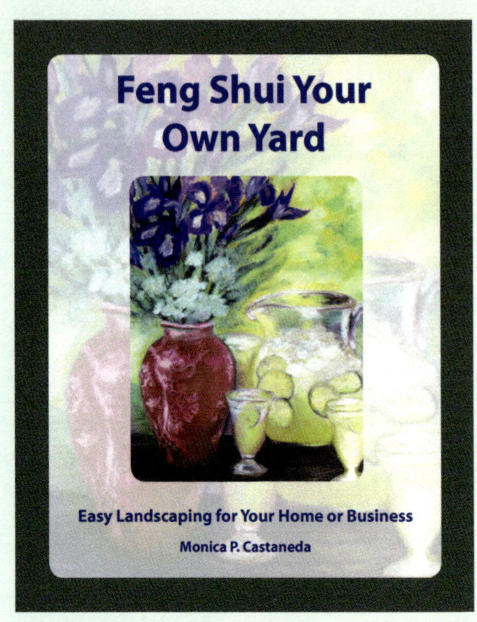

Feng Shui Your Own Yard
Easy Landscaping for Your Home or Business

Feng Shui Your Own Life Areas
Room by Room

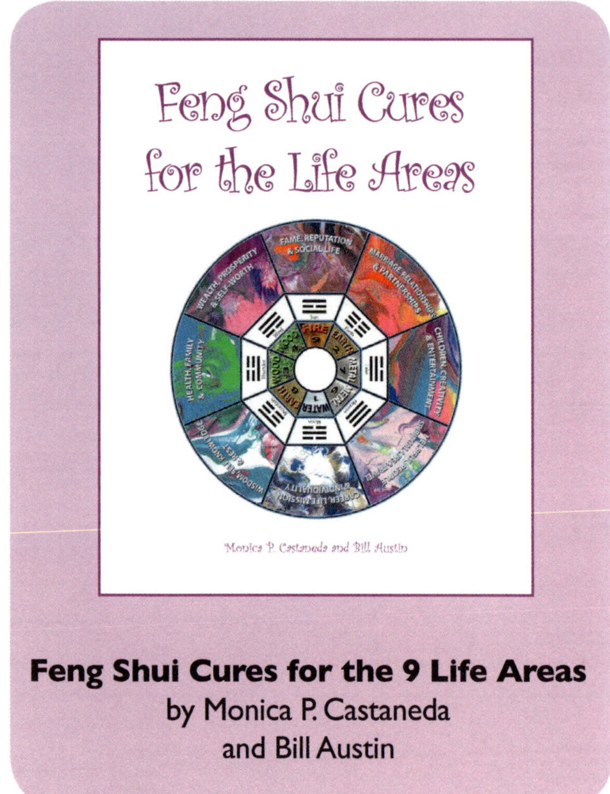

Feng Shui Cures for the 9 Life Areas
by Monica P. Castaneda
and Bill Austin

fengshuiforus.com/books.html

36287231R00076

Made in the USA
Charleston, SC
27 November 2014